MW00900618

Children's Ministry
Moving Forward

Shannon + Adam
Love You friends !! :)
Thanks for all you've
done for the Kingdom,
and for me !! ♡

Esther R. Thomer

P.S. Check out
page #34 ☺

Children's Ministry Moving Forward

A Healthy Kidmin Perspective

Esther Moreno

Copyright © 2019 by Esther Moreno.

ISBN:	Softcover	978-1-9845-7160-1
	eBook	978-1-9845-7159-5

All rights reserved. No part of this book may be reproduced or transmitted in any form or by any means, electronic or mechanical, including photocopying, recording, or by any information storage and retrieval system, without permission in writing from the copyright owner.

Any people depicted in stock imagery provided by Getty Images are models, and such images are being used for illustrative purposes only.
Certain stock imagery © Getty Images.

Print information available on the last page.

Rev. date: 12/12/2018

To order additional copies of this book, contact:
Xlibris
1-888-795-4274
www.Xlibris.com
Orders@Xlibris.com
789501

To Guylando, Grace, and Gideon who set my passion for the next generation ablaze through their constant love and support.

CONTENTS

ACKNOWLEDGEMENTS

*"I can do things you cannot, you can do things I
cannot. Together we can do great things."*
-Mother Teresa

Every accomplishment that I have ever achieved has been the direct result of the investments of those around me. I will never forget, as I started my journey in Children's Ministry, all those individuals who decided to take a chance on me. Through all the triumphs and missteps, and there were many, these people believed in me and saw something in me at the time I didn't see in myself. I thank the multitude of friends, educators, pastors, authors, and family members who have made major contributions into my life.

Thanks to my parents Michael and Janice Miller who had me. Great team work guys! Also, to my siblings Michael, Lydia, and Madalyn who have remained some of my biggest cheerleaders to this day.

Thanks to my colleague, mentor, and dear friend Ricardo Miller of Ricardo Miller Ministries who continues to inspire me to reach for the stars without restraint.

Special thanks to my brilliant husband, Guylando Moreno, who worked tirelessly at editing this book. He and our two beautiful children, Grace and Gideon, continue to be the driving force behind all that I do. Their patience and support have enabled me to expand my impact in reaching the next generation and for that I am eternally grateful.

FOREWORD

I believe one of the most important roles in a church is the Children's Pastor/Director. Churches that are thriving usually have a thriving Children's Ministry. And a thriving Children's Ministry is led by a passionate leader.

I am excited for this book to get into the hands of churches and Children's Ministries across the country and around the world. It is grounded not just in theory, but in proven experience by my friend, Esther Moreno.

Esther is a thriving, high-energy, exciting leader who is living the principles found in this book. I've had the honor to partner with her on several ministry outreaches and conferences. She is a great example of what you're going to read.

In this book, Esther shares not only a winning philosophy for Children's Ministry, but the practical nuts and bolts it takes to build a thriving Children's Ministry. The truths she shares aren't usually found in a college classroom, but in the wisdom that comes from serving in Children's Ministry for years.

I am excited to see this book in the hands of Children's Ministry leaders. It will infuse them with fresh ideas, principles, and insights that work. It will help Children's Pastors/Directors forge a solid pathway into the future.

You've probably heard this quote before. It rings true for Children's Ministry as well. *"Everything rises and falls on leadership."* As you grow as a leader, your ministry will grow. This book will help you grow. It will challenge you. It will inspire you. It will stretch you. It will take you out of your comfort zone...and that's a good thing. Nothing grows in your comfort zone. But as you read this book and see Children's Ministry leadership through a challenging perspective, you will grow and your ministry will grow. Get ready to go to the next level.

- Dale Hudson, Founder
  Building Children's Ministries

INTRODUCTION

For years I have been obsessed with theme parks! Why? Because I love rollercoasters! The bigger the rollercoaster, the better! I will never forget the day I mustered up the courage to sit at the very front of one. It was the most terrifying experience of my life. I can remember the pit in my stomach as we got higher and higher to the peak of the slope. Even now I can hear the clinking noise of the rails as we climbed past each track. I can recall a defining moment in my life when I had reached the top and decided to do the unthinkable. I lifted my arms high in the air and opened my eyes as wide as I could. Those seconds that followed my decision were the longest and most exhilarating seconds of my life. My journey in Children's Ministry has been no different. Like many of you who are reading this right now, it has been filled with highs and lows. However, in the midst of it all, it has been one of the most exhilarating experiences of my life. I pray the same is true for many of you.

In this book I have chosen to focus on 7 core topics. These topics include: Knowing Yourself, Knowing your Audience, Being Prepared, Owning your Call, Understanding the Times, Engaging Technology, and Breaking the Mold. I believe that whether you are the leader of a Children's Ministry department, or serving as a Children's Ministry worker in your local church, mastering these 7 areas will revolutionize the way you see ministry and will dramatically change the type of results you are currently experiencing. The information in this book should not be considered methods. They are universal principles that will work, if applied. It is my hope that this will not be a one read book for you. In fact, it's a book you should read more than once to ensure you capture the truths within it. In this book you will discover the important and necessary journey of discovering self. You will learn why it's so important to know your audience and be prepared. You will be encouraged to update yourself on what's current. You will be challenged to own your call and become the uncommon leader that stands above the crowd.

Even though this book comes from my perspective, I am grateful for the veteran voices that have challenged me throughout the years and have contributed to the leader I am today. I continue to glean and learn from them as we journey together through the great world of Kidmin. Wherever you are in your journey remember this...

Info received and not applied is useless

...Now let's begin.

CHAPTER 1

Know Yourself

Discovering You

"Where is he?" the people began to mutter. The Israelites' request for a king had finally been answered only their king was nowhere to be found. Still not confident in his new found role as a leader, there he stood, hunched down low and cowering among the baggage. Even after continuous confirmations of his calling, it remained hard for Saul to wrap his mind around the fact that he was a king. He just couldn't believe it!

Like many of us today, Saul struggled with fully embracing his new role because he just didn't know who he was. I imagine as he was hiding, the two sided conversation in his head went like this: Okay, this is crazy! I can do this. I can't do this! I'm only me. Come on man, act like a king! How am I going to lead these people? What if they don't like me? What if I mess up? What if I really mess up?!

I shared a similar experience when I started my journey in Children's Ministry. I'll never forget the incredible feeling I felt when I was called to my first church as the Children's Ministry Director. I glowed with pride as I was informed, along with the rest of the congregation, of the unanimous decision to bring me on board out of a slew of other candidates. Yes! I knew that I was certainly called for this position and

I received confirmation from more than two or three witnesses. After the excitement had worn off and the reality of the responsibilities began to pile up, the intimidation and insecurities began to sink in. Sure, I wanted to take this position by the horns and really own it. Besides, out of all the people God could have chosen, he chose me. But because I didn't know myself, I constantly struggled with my own weaknesses rather than focusing on the amazing possibilities of how God could use uniquely-designed me to take the church's children's department to another level.

Embracing Self

I believe one of the biggest mistakes that many of us make as Children's Ministry Leaders is not taking out the appropriate time to truly discover self. Instead of embracing our God given roles as next generation leaders and remaining vigilant at personal growth and self-discovery, we simply try to play the part of whatever is expected of us. The only problem with that is, at the hint of any sign of criticism or discouragement, we are questioning our calls, crying woe is me, and hiding among the baggage, or at least our desks (which I've done before by the way)! So do you know who you are? True, we all may not be kings but inside of us all is something great that God has birthed in us for his glory. Your job is to go on a journey of self-discovery to figure out what that is, then completely own it like no one's business. No Children's Ministry Leader can truly be successful without first knowing self. You have to know who you are, accept who you are, and love who you are before you can effectively lead others.

Embracing Weaknesses

For years as a Kidmin leader I invested the majority of my energy into improving in those areas where I was weak while completely ignoring the areas where I truly shined. Part of the journey of discovering self is learning your strengths and weaknesses. For instance, it turns out that I'm a pretty good speaker and both kids and adults flock to me as a result. It also turns out that I'm pretty lousy at organization. I have the bobby pins, purple crayon, and old curriculum pouring out of my file cabinet to prove it. Now I get it. Nobody wants to highlight the areas where they may struggle. When you go in for a job interview, no person in their right mind when asked tell me about yourself responds with, "Well...let me tell you what I'm horrible at first." No way!

Know this one fact: Everyone has weaknesses. To truly know ourselves, we must take a deep look in the mirror and identify those weaknesses head on! Take a personal assessment. If you don't know what you're particularly weak in, be bold enough to ask those who love you enough to tell you the truth. But don't ask that jealous cousin whose response may or may not be a little biased. Don't be intimidated by this process. Remember, we're on a journey of self-discovery. Not being able to identify your weaknesses can be detrimental to your Children's Ministry department because it does three things. First, it robs your Children's Ministry Department of being the best it can be. Second, it robs those around you out of a valuable ministry opportunity. Third, it robs you.

We Rob Our Children's Ministry Department

When people desire to excel, they naturally focus on making those weaker areas in their lives better. You've heard it before. In the New Year I'm going to be more organized. I'm going to work out. I'm going to be better at "fill in the blank." Even though that's not a bad thing, when we exert all our energy focusing on what we're bad at, then we tend to neglect the areas where we excel. I will never forget the intimidation I experienced after accepting a Kidmin position where the prior director was a spreadsheet master! She had a spreadsheet for everything, including attendance records, programming, special events, mission projects, and curriculum!

I was determined to prove myself just as strong as my predecessor, if not stronger. The only problem was that I was terrible at spreadsheets!

When I finally learned how to create a spreadsheet, my eyes would go cross over all of the little details. This deficiency was not lost on the other church leaders who were quick to point out my frequent spreadsheet shortcomings. Their acknowledgement of my flaws ironically strengthened my resolve to prove that I could excel in an area where I had zero natural aptitude. Instead of wisely delegating the task to someone who possessed the skills to do it in 20 minutes or less, I wasted hours to complete it myself. This futile attempt to strengthen a weakness caused me to neglect the very strengths that made me, me. The same strengths that got me hired in the first place.

We Rob Those around Us Out of a Ministry Opportunity

When we continue to take on tasks in Children's Ministry that we are not good at, we take valuable ministry opportunities away from those who are good at those tasks. It is painful to see someone struggling to perform a task when there are others who are ready, willing, available, and better equipped to take on the role. I cannot tell you the countless times I have witnessed this and just cringed.

I will never forget watching a children's pastor completely ruin the most valuable part of a kids' event. I knew there were other people available who were gifted at drama who would jump at the chance to lead that valuable part of the program if asked. I thought to myself, why are you doing this when you suck at it? This is the most important part. It's the main point! At the end of the day, it was clear to most of the children and all those serving as volunteers for the event that acting was not her strong suit, but she continued to do this part of the program year after year!

This leader clearly did not identify or embrace their weaknesses well. The funny part is that this person was good at so many other things. By not stepping down and allowing someone better to do this particular role, they not only robbed someone from a ministry opportunity but in so doing they exchanged a role that could have been dynamic in exchange for mediocrity. Being willing to step aside and allow a superior performer to assume a role is not a failure or a shortcoming, but a mark of true leadership. No person is the same and God has equipped us all with different gifts for the purposes of his glory. This point is expressed in the book of Exodus Chapter 31 as the children of Israel are building the Tabernacle:

> *Then the Lord said to Moses, "See, I have chosen Bezalel son of Uri, the son of Hur, of the tribe of Judah, and I have filled him with the Spirit of God, with wisdom, with understanding, with knowledge and with all kinds of skills— to make artistic designs for work in gold, silver and bronze, to cut and set stones, to work in wood, and to engage in all kinds of crafts.*

Exodus 31:1-5 (New International Version)

Wow. God had a job that needed to get done and anointed certain individuals with special abilities to get that job done the right way. Can you imagine Moses saying, "Thanks a lot God, but I got this!" and investing the majority of his time learning how to make furniture? Anything that Moses produced would have inevitably been far inferior to the work of Bezalel, the God-appointed craftsman. Even though it sounds kind of silly, we are guilty of doing this in Children's Ministry when we refuse to delegate tasks we are not strong in to those God has gifted to handle it. Remember, it's not our Children's Ministry. It's his. Just like the body of Christ, our Children's Ministries are made up of different parts that all work together with different roles to make the department as a whole great.

We Rob Ourselves

We do ourselves a huge disservice when we overly invest in the areas where we are weak instead of delegating those tasks to others who are stronger or better equipped to fulfill them. In so doing, we not only exhaust ourselves but rob others of the opportunity to truly shine their God given abilities. For one, we end up carrying unnecessary loads we were never meant to bear. For instance, one year I had made it my responsibility to completely prepare the entire curriculum for each class in our Children's Ministry. This was an effort to provide my leaders with as much convenience as possible. Despite multiple offers of support from those around me, I stubbornly committed myself to this self-imposed task that distracted me from more crucial responsibilities. So there I was sitting at my desk cutting small pieces of chains for an arts and craft project like a ding dong head wasting what could have been a productive day in the office.

I am happy to report that I eventually came to my senses and delegated the task to a woman who was waiting to be asked to do it and actually found pleasure in prepping each and every Sunday. I am so grateful for my delegation epiphany because it not only saved me countless hours, but allowed me to engage a fantastic leader who was hungry to serve. This is what happens when we don't use those around us properly. We also end up with unhealthy skeleton crews in our Children's Ministries because when people feel like they aren't being used properly or at all, they will leave. When people notice you have a skeleton crew, they will be drawn away from serving in the Children's Ministry because no one wants to join a sinking ship. Get my point! Embrace weaknesses and delegate accordingly. I promise you will be much happier.

Be the Best Version of You

At the end of the day, just because you're not awesome at everything doesn't mean pending doom! Guess what! There are so many people around you that are good at the things you aren't! Find these people, nurture them, and they will become some of your greatest assets in developing a successful Children's Ministry. Yes, that means you don't have to be perfect! You're allowed to be you, weaknesses and all. Don't you feel so much better now! Now don't get me wrong; I'm not saying embrace all of your strengths and throw caution to the wind when it comes to your weaknesses. But in order to maximize our purpose, we must be continually committed to becoming the best version of ourselves. It is possible that something you may not be good at now, through hard work and discipline, can become one of your strengths later.

Know Your Strengths

So what are your strengths? Do you know them? I mean really know them? Part of discovering who you are is identifying those areas in which you naturally thrive. Your strengths are what make you, well...you! It's what sets you apart from all the other billions of humans walking the earth. Part of why so many of us struggle with recognizing our strengths is because we're so busy comparing ourselves to those around us. But if we focus too much on what others are doing or how they are excelling, then we tend to overlook or under-appreciate the strengths we do possess.

This was definitely one of my struggles. It seemed that every ministry that I worked for seemed to have the same thing to say about me. "She is so enthusiastic," they would say. Don't get me wrong. I didn't mind being identified as a little enthusiastic. Besides, I loved my job in Children's Ministry. After the first few times, it was a term of endearment. But after the 10th, 11th, and 12th time hearing it, it was starting to get a little old. When someone introduces you as super enthusiastic (and nothing else) after a labor intensive week in Children's Ministry, it can start to feel downright offensive. I thought to myself, don't they know what I do and the work I put in around here to create a great experience for their kids on Sunday, and all they can say is that I'm enthusiastic!

I was so busy wanting them to say that I was amazing at all things pertaining to the daily operations of Children's Ministry, that I completely missed an honest acknowledgment of one my greatest strengths. It wasn't a failure to acknowledge my other accomplishments, it was just that my "enthusiasm" so eclipsed the other traits that it was the most notable to those who observed me. After getting my head out my butt and getting over myself, I realized to my delight that I was extremely enthusiastic and still am. I possess a glow and bubbly personality that has a way of lighting up any dark space. I am passionate about Christ, and zealous at making him known to children. I am eager to do whatever I need to do to make something great. I have an energy that pumps up the crowd and leaves children on the edge of their seats.

Part of becoming you is learning what you're really good at and owning it. Only after I acknowledged and owned my strength of enthusiasm was I able to channel it more effectively for the glory of God. So what's your dormant strength waiting to be unleashed on the world? Don't just assume who you are now is who you're meant to be forever. Remember, all strengths aren't readily apparent or fully developed. It's only as we discover self, or more precisely the strengths God has equipped us with, that we are able to embrace them and fan into flame those hidden treasures that lie beneath the surface.

Every strength people possess is not the same, so don't waste your time comparing. For instance, I have a friend in Children's Ministry who definitely doesn't share my strength in enthusiasm but can make a children's space come alive like nobody's business. Yet another skill that I do not possess. I could try to do it but somehow my dollar store feather boas and stick people pictures just don't cut it.

The whole point is to continually commit yourself to becoming the best version of you. In so doing, you learn what you're great at. The more you discover your strengths, the more you will attract other people who have discovered theirs as well. Surrounding yourself with individuals who know their strengths will only serve to sharpen and lead you down a road to even more self-discovery. Conversely, when you don't know who you are, it's natural to be more comfortable around others who don't know who they are. But if that's you, I encourage you to fight the temptation and begin to identify positive people who are confident.

Choose to be around people that serve to make you better rather than more comfortable. Trust me. It will be worth it. The healthiest Children's Ministry teams are led by people who have discovered who they are and who they are not. They recognize that a strong team consists of a diverse set of people who aren't all the same, but rather have different strengths and abilities that result in strengthening our Children's Ministry departments. In fact, the more diverse, the better.

One of the greatest tragedies in Children's Ministry today happens when we ignore the strengths of those around us because we have allowed the "fill a slot" mentality to guide our leadership decisions. This distorted mindset never works and only leads to weak teams filled with people in the wrong spots, wrong ministry, and one discouraged Children's Ministry leader. Everyone suffers when this approach is taken, especially the children and the parents who have entrusted their children into our care for spiritual growth and guidance.

3 Ways to Discover Your Strengths

Passion

What are you passionate about? I mean really passionate about? What's that thing that gets you going and when you get started you just find yourself getting lost in it? No, I'm not talking about your secret pipe dream to be a singer on American Idol when your singing skills are mediocre at best. I'm talking about that thing that just seems to be your niche' that you fall into with ease. Maybe it's being in front of people or maybe it's working behind the scenes to make something great. Whatever it is, lean into it.

Don't presume that something isn't a strength simply because it doesn't come naturally to you. Quite often the things that we are really strong in are in direct contrasts to our fears. Some of the best speakers I have heard that seemed to flow with ease have admitted to me their very real struggle with stage fright. So be encouraged and don't give into fear. Pray to God to help you push pass the fear so that you can be all that he's called you to be.

Effectiveness

Think you've pinpointed those passions and strengths of yours? Let's make sure they are really your strengths and not your imagination going wild after that bean burrito you had the other day. Take a deeper look at the effectiveness factor meaning when you operate in that so called gifting, are you effective? Do you see the atmosphere around you improve or change for the better? Does your strength -- when activated -- help those around you? If it doesn't, then it may not be your strength. However, if it does, you may have come one step closer to discovering you.

Strength Tests

There are a variety of tests and evaluations available to you at the click of a mouse if you really struggle pinpointing those areas of strength in your life. Most of them consist of questions regarding your preferences, likes, and desires, which are then tabulated into a list of likely strengths to consider. It's not fool proof, but if you're like me it's definitely a start to discovering your hidden talents and I highly recommend you take one if you haven't before. These are just a few to get you started but the available resources are endless:

> *https://gifts.churchgrowth.org/spiritual-gifts-survey*
> *https://spiritualgiftstest.com/*
> *https://mintools-store.com/products/spiritual-gifts-tests*
> *www.buildingchurch.net/g25.htm*
> *www.ubpcshape.org*

Also consider asking the pastor or ministry leaders at your local church for guidance in this area. I am sure that they will be more than willing to point you in the right direction.

Key Insights

❖ You have to know who you are, accept who you are, and love who you are before you can effectively lead others.

❖ Everyone has weaknesses. Figure out yours and delegate accordingly.

❖ Be willing to step aside and allow a superior performer to assume a role. Remember, it is not a failure or a shortcoming to step aside, but a mark of true leadership.

❖ Never underappreciate your strengths! Embrace and fan into flame those hidden treasures that lie beneath the surface.

❖ Avoid the comparison game. It is a waste of time!

❖ Choose to be around people that serve to make you better rather than more comfortable.

❖ In order to discover your strengths, consider those areas where you are both passionate and effective. Consider taking an assessment or talking to your local pastor or ministry leader for more guidance in this area.

CHAPTER 2

Know your Audience

"What are you wearing!?" My twin sister said to me in shock, and with what I would consider to be a little disgust. I didn't get it. Besides, I thought I looked fine. At the predominantly white "come as you are" non-denominational church I worked for at the time, it was the cat's meow! But apparently what I thought was a trendy outfit was a major fashion faux pas! It wasn't long until she reminded me that I was speaking in front of a predominantly black conservative congregation who wore big church hats, three piece suits, the works. Then it hit me. Oh my gosh, she was right! I can't wear this! I had made the epic mistake of not knowing my audience and I was in a code red emergency! So how did I handle it? I did what any good sister would do. I guilted her into switching outfits with me and the day was saved! My talk went great and my message was received. So what's my point? Knowing your audience is critical if you want to be successful in Children's Ministry.

When we don't take out the time to know our audience, we risk our messages falling flat. This is especially important when your message is the hope giving, life changing, word of God! This is a message we definitely want our children to hear. And if you want them to hear it in a way that they will receive it, then it is crucial that you know the type of children you are ministering to week after week. So do you KNOW

YOUR AUDIENCE? I will never forget a good friend of mine sharing with me his horror story of not knowing his audience.

On a mission's trip to Mexico, he was given the opportunity to minister to children in the community at a special event. Of course, as a Children's Pastor, my friend jumped at the chance to be a blessing and share a life giving word to those kids who were in attendance. However, what he didn't realize is that a lot of the children in the audience were street kids. If you don't know what "street kids" are, they are homeless children who were not able to secure a position in the local orphanages and are subject to live on the streets under what many would consider extremely impoverished conditions. Can you imagine the look of horror on my friend's face when he discovered that this uplifting message on the importance of gratitude for our homes and loving families was delivered to street children who were lucky enough if they got their hands on a piece of bread that day. Talk about wanting to curl up in a ball and die. As horrible as this story may sound, we do the same thing week after week in our Children's Ministries when we don't take out the time to know our audience.

Demographics

Do you know and understand the demographics surrounding the children who show up in your Children's Ministries? Do you truly understand the challenges that face the people you minister to week after week? I believe one of the biggest mistakes a church can make is not being intentional in obtaining the necessary statistical data needed to maximize total effectiveness. You're not going to open up a young and trendy clothing shop in a community full of senior citizens. Even though your store may be top of the line, you're likely to receive very few customers because the business wasn't tailored to fit the basic needs of that community. The same is true for church. In many instances, the church can be referred to as a business model. This is something a lot of people fail to accept. Spirit is vital but practicality is just as important. Contrary to popular belief there is a business side to ministry.

I know that's a hard pill to swallow for many of my religious friends. However, I assure you, that any church that's crushing it has an executive pastor and is operating under a business model that is allowing them to thrive. As Kidmin leaders, we are running the most important business in the world! We are in the business of saving souls and the CEO of our company is Jesus Christ of Nazareth. We are selling a product that isn't perishable, but one that has the power to change and transform the lives of children. So if we live in an area that is economically depressed, where the children are regularly confronted with a lack of food, shelter, or parental oversight, then we need to tailor our children's ministries to address those basic needs. Conversely, if we live in an area that is generally affluent, then our messages need to be framed in such a way that deals with the challenges that accompany wealth and the lack of exposure it often breeds. Tailoring our message to particular audiences is not a new invention. In fact, the Apostle Paul was a master at understanding his demographic and leveraging it for the glory of God.

> To the Jews I became like a Jew, to win the Jews. To those under the law I became like one under the law (though I myself am not under the law), so as to win those under the law. To those not having the law I became like one not having the law (though I am not free from God's law but am under Christ's law), so as to win those not having the law. To the weak I became weak, to win the weak. I have become all things to all people so that by all possible means I might save some.

1 Corinthians 9:20-22 (New International Version)

Paul was extremely intentional at understanding the demographics of the communities in which he ministered, and so should we. Paul was a student of the culture and the Word. By understanding both the will of God and the context in which he operated, Paul was masterful at tailoring the message to the needs of the hearer. When in Corinth, he referenced the Isthmian games and used athletic analogies to further highlight his message. While surrounded by Greek philosophers, he drew their attention to the unknown God. Even when he was in prison, he referenced his roman citizenship to elevate his platform and gain audience with higher tribunals. The point is that Paul married the message with the mindset of the audience in order to gain maximum impact for the gospel.

When it comes to our Children's Ministries, we should be doing the same thing. So are you culturally sensitive to the ethnic backgrounds of the children that encompass your Children's Ministry? Have you been intentional at understanding the specific family structures of the children that you serve? For example, how many children in your ministry come from single parent homes? Do you know how many children have been touched by the sting of divorce or have emerged from the foster care system? If your answer to most of these questions is "I don't know," then consider this your homework assignment. I will never forget this incredibly special boy I met at one of the children's church services I led. He looked very dapper as he came up to the table in his bow tie. A woman that I assumed was his mother came up to the table with him to sign him in. She too was dressed very well and was extremely friendly. As the young man went in and they parted ways, she felt the need to caution me about a few things.

She began to explain to me how this young man was not her son but that she was his aunt. She then went into a heartbreaking story about the boy's mother who had made it very clear to her and the young man that she no longer wanted him. Of course, as one would suspect, he was devastated. Despite the young man's multiple attempts to return back to his mother, she would not budge on her decision and threatened to throw him into the foster care system if other family members didn't step in immediately. With tears in her eyes, she had asked me to keep an eye on him and to let her know if I had any problems. In that moment, this woman had given me the greatest gift she could have ever given. It was the gift of understanding.

When you know where the children in your children's ministry are coming from and what they are going through, you respond differently.

I am happy to report, that I had no problems with that young man that afternoon because I knew based off of his background, the immediate needs he had so I went to town! Before that young man left, I loved on him like crazy! I constantly shared with him how personally happy I was that he was spending his time with us. I also made it a point for him to walk away knowing that he was immensely loved by God and accepted just as he was. Now I get it. It is impossible to know every personal detail, family history trauma, or prior challenge that the children within your ministries have endured. Yet even knowing the basic demographics of your audience will greatly aid you in tailoring your message accordingly.

Learning Styles

One frequently overlooked demographic is learning styles. So I want you to take a moment and create a picture in your head of what an average day in children's programming may look like for you. I want you to think about the diverse group of children that you interact with. Maybe you have those super active twins who stampede into the classroom full of anticipation to get a preview of the day's lesson, or more likely, activity. We can't forget about that girl or boy who is super timid and silently watches the behavior and interactions of all the other kids. They want to be active, but still feel a little too unsure of themselves to really take the plunge. Then we have the infamous group of older rambunctious boys who think they're too cool for school. But don't worry about them because Tattletale Tanya is sure to let you know if any of them get too far out of line. And, of course, you can't forget that little girl who is obviously a member of the track and field club because she just won't stop running. Congratulations! Your job is to come up with an engaging lesson that reaches this very diverse group of children. No pressure, right! When it comes to kids, no child is a clone of another. All are uniquely designed. Even siblings from the same home all have their own thing that makes them unique and this includes learning styles.

When it comes to teaching children, there are generally three main learning styles: Kinesthetic, Auditory, and Visual. There's no magic formula or explanation on why a child learns best in one way while their friend learns best in another. But every Children's Ministry leader would be well served to master teaching techniques that effectively minister to each of these of these learning styles. It is certainly a best practice to consider all three of these learning styles when preparing a service for children. Failure to do so may mean that some or a significant component of children within your classroom may feel left behind, bored, or completely uninspired. Now don't panic if you have not been doing this. A little tweak here, and a little creativity there, will go a long way in creating a message that is sure to pop in the hearts and minds of every child. So if this is your first time learning about these styles, then this is the time to grab your favorite highlighter and go to town. So let's go!

Kinesthetic Learners

Kinesthetic learners are those kids who shoot their hands up right away when you say, "Can I have a volunteer?" They love being active, moving around, and will take any opportunity to do so. These are your movers and shakers. They like to touch things in order to learn about them and have a preference for more experiential learning opportunities. Case in point, they like to move. That's right! Kids can learn while moving. I've been in a classroom before chocked full of children where the only child who could properly answer the Bible review question was the child who just couldn't keep still. Unfortunately, when it comes to kinesthetic learners, these learners are often mistaken for as the "bad kids" in classroom settings. It is crucial that we use discernment and never label children based upon our own frustrations, but do what we can to reach the heart of every child. I know when we work tirelessly at preparing quality lessons for children, it is a temptation to want the children to sit still and quietly listen. Even though I am a firm believer that kids should be taught not to talk while the teacher is talking, I don't believe that children should be forced to sit still for an extended amount of time. I have witnessed leaders in Children's Ministry repeatedly discipline specific children with the so called "jitters" during Children's Ministry events. "Billy, if you don't sit still, you won't get any candy!" The only problem is that Billy has been forced to sit and listen to a 30-minute message when the average attention span for a child is less than 7! By the way, if you're in Children's Ministry and you do that… DON'T! I've sat through those messages, and they are grueling to watch, and I'm a grownup!

So question time! Who are your movers and shakers? Have you really been intentional in reaching them where they are, or have you been trying to shove them into a box of who you want them to be? Are you wondering what you can do to meet your jitterbugs where they are and create a message that lasts? Remember, kinesthetic learners love to move, so high energy worship will always help fit the bill. Also, when you are teaching a lesson and you need help from the audience, try to consider calling on those kids who you can discern are busting at the seams to get up and move. If you want to bring the Word of God to life for these learners, anything that involves physical activity will pay dividends, not only during your programming but in the spiritual health and growth of your children thereafter.

Auditory Learners

You can think of these types of learners as the classic old school teacher's pet. Auditory learners are the kids that likely benefit from traditional methods of teaching. These learners are often assumed to be "the good kids" because they always seem to be really engaged and listening intently to your message. Since their learning is tied more to their sense of hearing, they tend to get more out of a lecturing style of teaching, provided it is supplemented with a little gusto and vocal inflections to maintain interest. They are still children after all. These children prefer to read out loud rather than silently to themselves, so feel free to choose one of them to read the memory verse or main point to the class. You won't likely get any pushback from them when requesting volunteer participation. Auditory learners also retain information well through creative word patterns and love music. Try to turn the memory verse into a fun song and really get these children's engagement wheels turning.

Visual Learners

You've heard the saying that a picture is worth a thousand words. Well, for visual learners, a picture is probably worth twice that! Visual learners learn best when lessons are creatively illustrated. These learners probably constitute a large majority of the children that you minister to on Sundays. Visual learners prefer to see lessons demonstrated because for these learners seeing is believing! Visual learners won't grasp a message simply from you telling it to them like auditory learners. In order to make a message stick for this creative bunch, you must activate their sense of sight through engaging visuals.

I can't tell you how much I enjoy seeing Children's Ministry leaders post how they have transformed a space for their children's programming. I greatly admire those Kidmin leaders with the uncanny ability to go into a boring or basic classroom and bring it to life with props, decorations, and details that reinforce the ministry focus of the month. Visual learners thrive in these types of environments. So if you aren't doing this already, consider throwing some pizazz into your space. Also, as you look at your lesson, consider props that you can use to really make it come alive. One of the greatest misperceptions is that in order to make a lesson really pop, you have to spend a lot of money. So not true. I have made more than one lesson come alive with little more than a quick trip to the local dollar store or fishing expedition in the basement. Remember that today's trash could be tomorrow's treasure. So keep those eyes open and good luck!

Key Insights

* ❖ Always make it a goal to know your audience.
* ❖ When we don't take out the time to know our audience, we risk our messages falling flat.
* ❖ Don't ignore the business side of ministry. Spirit is vital but practicality is just as important. I assure you, any church that is crushing it has an executive pastor and is operating under a business model that is allowing them to thrive.
* ❖ Know the demographics of the children and families in your ministry. Consider visiting your local Children Services/Child Protection Agencies for information regarding needs within your community.
* ❖ It is impossible to know every personal detail, family history trauma, or prior challenge that the children within your ministries have endured. Yet even knowing the basic demographics of your audience will greatly aid you in tailoring your message accordingly.
* ❖ When it comes to kinesthetic learners, these learners are often mistaken for as the "bad kids" in classroom settings. Don't make that mistake!
* ❖ Be intentional in incorporating every learning style when creating a lesson for children. This includes Kinesetic, Auditory, and Visual learners.

CHAPTER 3

Be Prepared

"There are no secrets to success. It is the result of preparation, hard work, and learning from failure."
-Colin Powell

That's right! There are no secrets to success, just plain hard work that gets us from one goal to the next. This truth is just as applicable to Children's Ministry as anything else. Preparation is critical if we are to have successful Children's Ministries. In other words, when we fail to plan, we plan to fail. One of the greatest misperceptions about Children's Ministry is that it only requires a good heart and a love of God to be successful. Unfortunately, this couldn't be further from the truth. Even possessing certain giftings will not save the leader who fails to prepare.

I knew an amazingly talented woman before in ministry, so I was not surprised when she told me that she had received her first position as a Children's Ministry Director. I was above the moon happy for her as I knew she had a great personality, loved kids, was full of creative ideas, and had a knack for collaborating with others. Sounded like a great recipe for a quality Children's Ministry leader, or at least I thought.

You see, as talented as she was, she never prepared for anything and unfortunately the Children's Ministry she oversaw suffered severely as a result. Instead of building a team, she became a one-man band. Everything she did from Sunday mornings to special events all seemed to be poorly put together with very little planning ahead of time. Her brilliant ideas never came to life and she constantly struggled to keep teachers on her team. I wish that I could tell you that she learned from her mistakes and grew as a result into a dynamic leader, but that was not her story. With her weakness in preparation, she ultimately ended up resigning and leaving the area of Children's Ministry altogether. Case in point...PLANNING IS KEY!!!!

So where did my poor friend go wrong? Well for starters, she was LAZY! Clear and simple, Children's Ministry is HARD WORK and anyone who goes into it thinking otherwise should reconsider if that's the area they really want to pursue. Unfortunately, my friend's story is not unique. I have encountered numerous churches where the ministry to children is the last priority, which means effective preparation is lacking. These churches and volunteers often view the ministry as little more than a babysitting club, which is reflected in their absence of clear goals, effective teams, and meaningful growth among the children. Ever wonder why effective Children's Ministry leaders get extremely annoyed at the term "babysitter"? It's because every person who wholeheartedly serves in Children's Ministry knows we're not just babysitting children so the grownups can enjoy their Sunday experience in big people church. NO WAY!!! We're in the background building future mountain movers and world shakers for Christ! Does that sound easy to you? I haven't heard of any Children's Ministry leader that hasn't had to sacrifice at one point or another their time, sleep, or personal desires to make sure their children's programming went over without a hitch.

My husband frequently reminds me of an occasion where my preparation reached a fever pitch. Earlier in my Kidmin journey, I was called upon to lead an event that was to be the cornerstone of our summer programming. I was determined to transform the classroom that we had been using all summer into a Mexican-themed fiesta replete with streamers, piñatas, balloons, and little mariachi singers. It was at approximately 2:00AM when my now husband realized how dedicated I was in making the event a success. He constantly reminds me how his soul cried out to the Lord after a display we had worked on for a great deal of the evening completely fell apart right before it was time to call it quits. Luckily, we were able to save our display and it served its purpose right in the nick of time. Unfortunately, I can't speak to the success rate of the homemade piñatas that refused to break but you get my point. Children's Ministry can be hard work and it demands preparation if we are going to be successful.

Another one of the top reasons we fail in Children's Ministry, despite incredible amounts of hard work, is because we are not intentional in surrounding ourselves with a strong team of people. Put another way, one of the most critical preparatory steps anyone can take is cultivating a strong team that can come along side you to fulfill the ministry vision. Strong teams composed of diverse people with different strengths are at the heart of any thriving Children's Ministry. Have you ever heard the saying, "many hands make light work?" Well, many hands create a strong Children's Ministry department, and without them your Children's Ministry will be mediocre at best. Strong teams help to maximize your impact. So do you have a strong team behind you? Well if you don't, guess what…that's hard work too! But it is possible to build regardless of how big or small your ministry is, if you're willing to put in the work.

Preparation & Strong Teams

Having a strong team behind you is essential if you want a successful Children's Ministry. There are so many churches where the weight of an entire Children's Ministry rest on the shoulders of one or two individuals. Others still just assume that it is the responsibility of the pastor's wife to throw something together from time-to-time. But this is a dangerous misperception that has the unintended consequence of stifling the effectiveness of the ministry and burning out the already short list of leaders. If you have found yourself in the unenviable position of being the "lone Kidmin ranger," then one of your most important assignments is to cultivate a team to support you. A strong team helps you to carry the load and prepare for the future.

If you're starting at a volunteer count of "0", then building a team can seem like an impossible task, but it doesn't have to be. What I have found is that if you view Children's Ministry as the "least of all" ministries, then so will your volunteers. We must first be convinced that this is an investment well worth making, then we will begin to attract a team of others that follow suit. There is a ton of scholarship around the sustainable volunteer cultures, but I believe it all begins and ends with the leadership. If you appear to be desperate and stressed, then your ministry may be unintentionally scaring away potential quality volunteers. On the contarary, if you present a compelling vision for the future of the ministry, exude excellence via your preparation every Sunday, and are intentional in sharing this vision with others, then you will soon find that others will take notice.

Part of creating a compelling vision is helping your teammates realize that Kidmin preparation can be great fun. It's a great opportunity to share ideas, grow in community, and build strong and long lasting bonds with like-minded Kidmin lovers. In spite of the complaints I've heard from struggling Kidmin leaders, you are not the only one in your church who cares about children. A great mentor and friend of mine always says, "Someone is assigned to help you." And it's true. We see this principle at work countless times throughout the scriptures. Moses had the judges; David had Jonathan; and Paul had Barnabas. You are no exception. There are designated people that God has called to help you to develop a successful Children's Ministry. Our Heavenly Father is intimately aware of what you can handle; the needs of the children in your congregation; and the time constraints that we all face. He has also promised to not put more on you than you can bear. One of the greatest epiphanies I have had in my Children's Ministry journey is that our ministries do not begin and end with the children, but very much extend to the adults as well. We often fail to recognize that our recruitment of Kidmin volunteers may be the first steps that these men and women have ever taken in any ministry capacity.

By way of illustration, I will never forget my dear friend Kim. I met Kim during my first full-time ministry assignment, where I was responsible for strengthening a Children's Ministry that ranged from kindergarten through 6th grade. While the church had many thriving Children's Ministry activities, it lacked consistent Sunday morning programming for the older elementary aged children. After befriending Kim, the mother of one of my outspoken 6th grade students, I quickly realized that she had quite the aptitude for working with that age-group and a heart for seeing them grow in the Lord. Without even a second thought, I asked Kim if she would be willing to assist with the Sunday morning programming for the 5th and 6th grade group. Kim became one my most valuable volunteers. She jumped in heart first and not only spearheaded the Sunday morning programming, but helped to sustain a fledgling praise-dance ministry, kid's book club, and Wednesday night programming.

It wasn't until I was called to another church that I realized the impact that my simple invitation to serve had on Kim. At my going away party, she confessed that prior to my invitation to serve in the Children's Ministry that nobody had ever asked her to serve in ministry. What appeared to me to be little more than an invitation to serve meant so much more. For her, it was an awakening of purpose, realization of latent ministry gifts, and inspiration to invest in the next generation.

As ministers to children, we must see our work at cultivating teams as much more than just volunteer recruitment. You may very well be ministering to the adults in your congregation by being the first person to open their eyes to God's plan for their lives. Not every invitation to serve will be met with equal success. But don't be discouraged or grow weary in your efforts to amass an enduring Kidmin team if some of your invitations are met with rejection. We must always remember that it's ultimately God's ministry. He desires to see it flourish. That means you must leave the outcome to Him. Your job is to walk in faith and go get the people that God has already laid before you.

The preparation principle applies to individuals and teams. In order to prepare effectively, your teams will likely need to have a regular cadence of meetings. Strong teams normally meet at least once a month. In addition to the regular meetings, I've also witnessed teams meet quarterly for a retreat that lasts for the entire day. A team meeting normally consists of updates but that is not where it ends. It's an opportunity to come together, share praise reports, celebrate team members, and generate fresh new creative ideas on how to take your Children's Ministry to the next level. Strive to keep your meetings fresh. Always keep your members guessing! Incorporate fun team building exercises that help to build comradery among the members of your team.

The whole point is to motivate your team in fresh and new ways. And please don't make this lame! You're Kidmin leaders after all so go nuts; and whatever you do, remember, the more laughter the better! So happy building, and remember…Rome wasn't built in a day. Really…think about it. Do you know the work that goes into building a quality home? First you have foundation construction work, framing, installation of windows, doors, roofing, siding, electrical plumbing, underlayment, drywall, and insulation just to name a few. I didn't even mention when the unexpected happens. It's a lot of work! The same is true for building a strong Children's Ministry Team. It takes time to lay a quality foundation. It takes hard work and dedication to see a vision come to pass. And sometimes, when we least expect it, the unexpected happens that has the ability to shake us at our core and make us feel like we're starting back at square one. People disappoint us, events don't turn out the way we planned, hurtful criticism comes from those we highly esteem. But I urge you to stick with it and always commit to growing a healthy team.

Preparation & Vision

And the Lord answered me and said: "Write the vision, and make it plain on tablets, That he may run who reads it. For the vision is yet for an appointed time

Habakkuk 2:2-3a (New International Version)

Planning and preparation should always stem from a greater vision that has been thoughtfully prepared, carefully analyzed, and written down. So what's a vision? Your vision is your end game, plain and simple. It identifies what you would like to achieve. What are the overall objectives of your Children's Ministry? What are the strategic actions you intend to implement to reach the goals? Vision is the ultimate safeguard that prevents you and your team from doing things with no meaning just for the sake of doing things because everything that you do in your Children's Ministry from Sunday mornings to special events is filtered through your ultimate vision. If it doesn't align with the ultimate vision of your Children's Ministry then off it goes! The vision serves as a roadmap for everyone to follow whether they are rocking babies in the nursery or wrangling in rambunctious 5th grade boys. Vision is the heartbeat that keeps your Children's Ministry going and the absence of it will cause your Children's Ministry to flat line.

> *"Where there is no vision, the people show up frustrated. Where there is no vision, the people have no discipline. Where there is no vision, the people loose motivation. Where there is no vision, the people perform like they don't care."*

-Ricardo Miller

So what's the vision in your Children's Ministry? Do you have one? Do you know it? Chances are, if you do have one and you don't know it, then it's time to review, refresh, and renew it. I am a firm believer that vision statements should be reviewed annually and tested in regards to impact. Also, consider potentially re-writing the vision when a new director of Children's Ministry is hired. You never know how God may want to use new leadership to take the ministry in a much needed different direction. So write the vision make it plain. Allow your vision to collide with your faith and unlock the door to a thriving Children's Ministry department.

Counting the Cost in Preparation

In Children's Ministry, we are constantly faced with decisions to make and new tasks to take on. With every decision we make, it is vital that we count the cost and prepare accordingly. There is a cost to everything that we do. If we fail to use wisdom and thoughtful contemplation, then our decision-making will be dictated by the cacophony of others' opinions instead of the original vision. Toward this end, church budgets are not limitless and it is God's desire that we are good stewards over what has been allotted to us. For this reason alone, we must be vigilant at counting the cost of every decision we make. I will never forget the first time I had to shop around for Children's Ministry curriculum. The curriculum that we were using would soon be discontinued so it was necessary to start shopping around for a new one. I began a report of all the curriculums I had researched for our program but it was no secret that I had my eye on one in particular. At the time, it was the hottest curriculum on the market and I finally had the opportunity to make it mine with little to no dispute. Even though it was a little pricey, I was convinced we needed to have it and had already prepared the perfect speech in the unlikely event I had to convince anyone otherwise. After receiving a sample of the curriculum, it wasn't long before I realized the immense work that had to go into appropriately preparing each Sunday's lesson. It was then that I began to question whether purchasing this curriculum was a good idea. As fancy as this curriculum would be, I was faced with the daunting task of counting the cost. How would my team respond having to review a 15 page lesson with intricate skits each week. I knew the answer was not well! Ultimately, I had to go with a less complex curriculum that would serve my group better and fit their own capacity to prepare. It was difficult letting my dream go, but I knew after counting the cost that I had made a wise decision that would ultimately benefit my team, the children, and the overall budget of the church.

Preparation vs. Wing-It Ministries

Recall the young woman that I mentioned at the start of this chapter; the one whose laziness frequently prevented her from exceeding in Children's Ministry. To be clear, it wasn't just pure laziness that was her problem. Rather it was the all too easy tendency to rely on her natural gifts and talents instead of properly preparing for the lessons that lay ahead of her. Undoubtedly, with very little effort she was able to make kids smile. In fact, she was a regular kid magnet. While this natural talent was great, it was no substitute for true preparation. If only she had paired her natural talent with necessary preparation, her lessons would have truly soared. But instead she would rush in every Sunday to briefly review her lesson immediately before the kids started to flood her room. Rather than using those moments to connect with them, she ignored them so that she could have five additional minutes to quickly scan through the curriculum. Instead of utilizing exciting props, media presentations, or inspirational skits, which is often the things kids remember, she had to rely on her engaging reading skills.

Just because preparation is necessary does not mean that it is easy. Nevertheless, it is the level and extent of preparation that separates truly excellent Children's Ministries from mediocre ones. Those leaders that are willing to do their homework, gather the necessary resources, and rehearse their messages are the same ones who most effectively inspire the next generation. This level of preparation is not exclusively reserved for larger churches, but is available to anyone who is willing to roll up their sleeves and make the Kidmin magic happen. For those who serve directly with kids in their Children's Ministry department, know that this level of preparation will most certainly vary from church to church, but generally has common threads:

1. It includes a preliminary review of the lesson to identify the necessary resources, props, and activities that are required to make the lesson come to life.
2. It means rehearsing or practicing the lesson in view of your audience. Preparing a lesson for preschool students will vary

greatly from the way that a similar message will be presented to older elementary aged children.

3. To the extent there are other teachers, then there should be a division of labor and alignment of overall responsibilities.

Of course, the inclusion of praise and worship, games, audio visual or digital features will again require additional time to ensure all of the features are executed according to the plan. While this may initially seem exhausting, if you are willing to make the investment of time and energy, the return is inspired children and it is INCREDIBLE!

Key Insights

❖ Don't believe the hype. A successful Children's Ministry takes hard work, sacrifice, and careful preparation. Be willing to put in the work and prepare.

❖ Don't be the "Kidmin lone Ranger" thriving Children's Ministries are dedicated to building strong teams.

❖ One of the most critical preparatory steps anyone can take is cultivating a strong team that can come along side you to fulfill the ministry vision. Strong teams composed of diverse people with different strengths are at the heart of any thriving Children's Ministry.

❖ Make sure you have a vision that is written out for your Children's Ministry department and shared with others. If you don't have one, get busy and write one today!

❖ With every decision we make, it is vital that we count the cost and prepare accordingly. There is a cost to everything that we do. If we fail to use wisdom and thoughtful contemplation, then our decision-making will be dictated by the cacophony of others' opinions instead of the original vision.

❖ Resist the temptation to wing it; review lessons, accumulate resources, and delegate appropriately ahead of time.

CHAPTER 4

Own It

Own Your Call

You got this and you were made for this! This is probably my favorite part of this book. It's the moment when I get the opportunity to drill into your brain that you are completely and totally awesome!!! You're a Kidmin leader, now I'm asking you to completely, unapologetically, and unabashedly OWN IT like it's nobody's business! You are currently working in the largest mission field in the world! I don't care what your role is in Children's Ministry. No job is too big or too small. Now get closer to the page and hear me when I scream this…WHAT YOU DO IS SIGNIFICANT!!!! Every week you help children who come from all walks of life to discover who they are in Christ. You're making imprints in their little brains that they are loved immensely by a God who is for them and not against them. You fill them with truth in a world of confusion and light in a world of darkness. You inspire them to walk in that truth boldly so that they may experience the fullness of God in every way in their lives. A fullness that is available to them right now. Does that sound unimportant to you?

Growing up, I used to be so impressed when I heard someone referred to as an evangelist. Whenever I would hear that "Evangelist" so and so was coming to town I would think to myself, "Man…that person is a big deal." Granted at that age, I didn't completely understand what the title really entailed, but in my Christian home it sounded super important. It wasn't until I got much older and began to walk in my calling that it occurred to me that I too was an evangelist. It was mind blowing. I am a child evangelist, and so are you. Every week whether you are greeting children at the door, changing poopie diapers in the nursery, or front and center giving the main message to children, you are reflecting the love of Christ and sending a message of hope to each and every child that graces your ministry. That's incredible. Now OWN IT!

One of the biggest reasons we don't own it when it comes to our roles in Children's Ministry is due to a lack of confidence in who we are and what we truly offer. Can you blame us? For years we have been labeled as babysitters and childcare providers. We've been trying to escape these titles forever, but there are so many churches out there that still cling to this outdated idea of Children's Ministry.

During my first official ministry position, I found myself in an office that wasn't even on the same floor as the rest of the staff. Literally, there was a wing of the building called "Staff." They should have called it "Entire staff except Esther," at least that's how I read it. My office was literally in a cold basement. To add insult to injury, there was a completely unused office available in the staff area that stayed empty until I protested to be moved into it. In another one of my Kidmin positions, I was told that it wasn't even necessary for me to attend the weekly staff meeting because I was hired as a part-time staff person with "a lot to do." Rather than acquiesce to my perceived subservient role, I made it my personal mission to be in every staff meeting! I thought to myself, are you kidding me?! I am a valuable member of this team, how dare you suggest I not be there.

Despite my initial zeal, I constantly struggled in that season with feelings of insecurity and questioned whether I had a place there. By the way, on a side note, if you are ever asked to be the face of a Children's Ministry department that doesn't require you to be in staff meetings, then BEWARE! You are the voice of the children and those who labor on their behalf. If you've ever heard of the saying "out of sight, out of mind," then that's what your Children's Ministry department will become to the senior leadership of your church if you are never a part of staff meetings. The whole point is, as Kidmin leaders, we are constantly faced with challenges that cause us to question our significance. It will inevitably happen, but we must be vigilant and stay the course.

One of the most encouraging gifts I ever received in ministry was from my friend Adam. At the time, Adam had served as the youth pastor of our church. One day Adam had apparently sensed that I was having a rough day in ministry, which was no surprise as we were friends. In an effort to brighten my day, Adam came to my desk and dropped off a small wooden plaque. It was nothing flashy but its inscription read, "My Boss Is a Jewish Carpenter." He explained to me that it was something that he always clung to when he was having rough days. He meditated on its importance whenever he questioned his calling, and now he felt the need to pass it on to me as he discerned that I too was questioning mine. In ministry there are some defining moments that you treasure in your heart for all time. This was one of mine. It reminded me that Jesus had called me to my position as a Kidmin leader. He was not surprised that I was where I was because he had placed me exactly where he wanted me to be. So are you.

As Children's Ministry leaders we must stand firm in our purpose, especially when we encounter situations that truly challenge us. One of the ways that I encourage myself is to declare the truth about the work I do and the investment I am making in the next generation. The truth is that we are focused on the most fruitful mission field in the world. The truth is that the impact that we are making is eternal. The truth is that our listeners' hearts are open and fertile to receiving the gospel. The truth is that the Father cares greatly about the hearts and minds of his little ones. The truth is that we are supernaturally empowered to accomplish the mission before us. The truth is that we offer rivers of living water in desserts of cultural darkness. The truth is we offer peace in a world of chaos. The truth is that one young soul may transform his or her generation. The truth is that when we are at our weakest with nothing left to give then God will nonetheless show himself strong to his little ones. The truth is that no matter how big or how small our ministries are, that we are changing the world one child at a time.

Own Your Failures

Now I want you to repeat after me: Everyone has failures! I don't care who you are. No one is immune to shortcomings and the faster you accept the fact that you're not going to win every time, the quicker you'll position yourself to be a better Children's Minister. In fact, I would argue that you're not qualified to lead if you've never failed. The best lessons in life are often learned through our failures. Unfortunately, it took me years to learn this. During my earliest days in the incredible world of Kidmin, you could say failure was my #1 hobby. It seemed as if my lack of experience resulted in almost constant mistakes. But instead of growing from those mishaps, I allowed every mistake that I had made as a Children's Minister to become a mental stronghold. Rather than walking in faith and setting really awesome goals for the ministry, I would constantly pull back in fear that I would fail yet again. Sure I knew how to talk a big game, but my fear always secretly kept me bound in "play it safe" mode. In other words, I regularly settled for maintaining instead of redefining my ministry space.

Despite my strongholds, I constantly did what I could to grow. I attended annual conferences as a way to strengthen my leadership abilities, but every time I got home and the conference zeal had faded I would find myself back at square one. This crazy cycle wasn't broken until I met my mentor and friend, Ricardo Miller, who challenged me to not be limited by my past but to rise above it. When he published the book, Wisdom Keys for Children's Ministry, I was eager to purchase a copy, but Ricardo insisted on personally delivering it to me as he happened to be in the area for prior engagements. Our family thoroughly enjoyed hosting Ricardo and of course he hand delivered the book, together with other goodies for my children. Yet the most memorable part of the day was the moment when Ricardo had left and I had a chance to thumb through my new Children's Ministry book. To this day, the personalized message that Ricardo penned has always stayed with me as a visible reminder of this important truth. The message read, "Accept your past without regret, handle your present with confidence and face your future without fear! The world needs what you have to offer!" Since that day, I have never viewed past failures in the same light; and if I do happen to reminisce on those past missteps, then I smile knowing that it is precisely those same failures that have made me the dynamic leader that I am today. And the same is true for you!

Owning Your Message

So how do you own your message? I have one word for you... AUTHENTICITY. We live in a world where authenticity is in short supply! No one wants to buy a vehicle from a greasy car salesman. Even if you walk away with a good deal you still feel like you got raked over the coals. Why? Because authenticity makes people feel comfortable. It causes people to let their guard down and opens them up to the heart of what we're trying to say. The same is true for Children's Ministry. If we want children and their families to truly receive the message we're giving, then we have to be authentic.

In Children's Ministries around the world, curriculum has been one of the most popular ways in which Kidmin leaders reinforce God's word to children. This has been both a blessing and a curse. The problem is that the influence is not in the curriculum. It's in the person giving the message. If that person is not prepared or confident in what they're saying, they may rely too heavily on the curriculum, and then: Boom! Dry message for one, please! I cannot tell you the number of times I've witnessed people take a quality curriculum and annihilate its effectiveness by leaning too heavily on it. Curriculum is like a skeleton. It serves as foundational material to help lead us to a main point. But it's up to us to put the meat on it. If we really want the message to stick, we have to own it.

I will never forget when my husband and I relocated to Chicago after a long stint in Ohio. As a Children's Minister I was so antsy to get involved in the local church. It was no surprise that after only three weeks of attending a church that I started volunteering in their Sunday school program. As part of my onboarding, I was designated to shadow the existing leaders in the elementary age class. As I entered the classroom, I immediately fell to the background and began observing in order to gain a better understanding of the culture of the space. When the time for the children's message arrived, my initial excitement ground to a halt when the "seasoned" leader climbed onto the stage and commenced boringly reading from the curriculum, which for all intents and purposes was glued to his hand. Staring even more intently at his script, this leader had lost not only my attention but every single child as he stumbled over every other word and re-read multiple sentences. Just when I thought that we had survived the worst of it, he turned the page! Despite his willingness to serve, this guy's inauthentic message fell on deaf ears

Talk about witnessing a train wreck in slow motion! If you work with children, then I am sure you know what happened next: their attention drifted and chaos ensued. This guy definitely did not own his message. In Children's Ministry it is of vital importance that you make the message yours, irrespective of whether you use an outside curriculum or create your own. Plain and simple; when we don't own our message, we lose impact. When I prepare a lesson, I make it a point to go through the curriculum ahead of time, extract the topic, and then pray over what it is God may be trying to speak to my heart concerning the main point. You would be surprised at how many "come to Jesus" moments I've personally experienced in preparing for a Sunday school lesson.

Preparing your lesson is not something that should be rushed the day of. I know that it is so easy to kick this can down the road, but I encourage you to resist the temptation to cram or procrastinate. The message of hope that we carry is a precious gift that shouldn't be taken lightly. It is important to make sufficient time to reflect on how the message speaks to you, which is absolutely necessary if you want to truly own it and make it yours. Thereafter, I place myself in the shoes of a child in an effort to convey the message in such a way that most resonates with them. I make it a point to not stop at the main lesson. When it comes to owning your message, it is important to make the message yours, the illustration yours, and even the music yours! Now I know that there's more than one way to skin a cat, and more than one way to own a message. My process is my process. Yours may look different. The whole point is to infuse your message with authenticity and watch little hearts and minds spring to life.

Own Your Time

It is so important that you own your time, particularly in Children's Ministry. If you are a people pleaser, then this is something you probably struggle with. People are always pulling for our time and if we're not careful, we can end up giving it away unnecessarily leaving us with very little time for the things that matter most. I can't tell you how many days I have left my church office at the end of the day asking myself, where did the time go? But if I am honest with myself, I know that I wasted my time on unfruitful activities and other distractions. Before I knew it, the clock had expired and it was time to turn back into a pumpkin. Freeing ourselves from the tyranny of distraction is one of the most important things that we as Children's Ministers can do. This truth is underscored in the parable of the four soils, wherein Jesus draws a parallel between four soils and fruitfulness in the lives of believers. The temptation to have days that are overscheduled, distracted, and filled with pursuing empty pleasures is characterized by the third soil that was full of weeds:

> *"A farmer went out to sow his seed. As he was scattering the seed, some fell along the path; it was trampled on, and the birds ate it up. Some fell on rocky ground, and when it came up, the plants withered because they had no moisture. Other seed fell among thorns, which grew up with it and choked the plants. Still other seed fell on good soil. It came up and yielded a crop, a hundred times more than was sown."*

Luke 8:5-8 (New International Version)

In examining this third soil, Jesus clarifies the meaning:

"The seed that fell among thorns stands for those who hear,
but as they go on their way they are choked by life's worries,
riches and pleasures, and they do not mature."

Luke 8:14 (New International Version)

These thorns (i.e., pleasures, concerns, or distractions) can limit or strangle the effectiveness of our ministries. So what does this look like? This looks like a young woman named Barb. Barb signed up for the choir, the PTA, the local exercise group, Wednesday night programming, Tuesday night book club, and a Friday night mom's group. But when it came time for her to prepare her Sunday school lesson, she was exhausted with little to nothing left to give. You may not be as over-scheduled as Barb, but you may need to do some spiritual gardening. What are the weeds and distractions in your life that may be strangling the purposes of God? While you most certainly can do all things through Christ, Christ has not called you to do all things. If you truly want to make an impact in the lives of the next generation, you must be discerning and judicious with the time afforded to you. There's only 24 hours in a day. Your time is a precious resource. Invest it wisely.

To be clear, I'm not saying that your commitment to Children's Ministry should be the sole and exclusive focus of your life. Your life is filled with non-negotiables that will often require your time over Children's Ministry. As the daughter of a pastor, I often witnessed the demands, pressures, and exhaustion that seem to chase those who are in full-time ministry. The failure to establish healthy boundaries is necessary. If you're not looking out for your family's wellbeing, then often times, no one is. When you're bombarded by demands, you have to prioritize constantly. Sometimes your family will have to take center stage, and at other times your commitment to Children's Ministry will.

The good news for us as believers is that we don't have to make these decisions alone. We have the blessed gift of the Holy Spirit to lead us and direct us as we walk through this life. I encourage you to make a realistic set of goals daily in an effort to protect your time. Practically, what this looks like for me is to set 10 main goals that I would like to accomplish before the end of the day. While some of the goals are directed towards my career, others are directed towards my home life including my own self-care. My 10th goal has stayed the same for some time now. I always write, "Don't beat yourself up if you don't hit all 10 goals!" The truth of the matter is that LIFE HAPPENS and sometimes our goals for the day get wiped out in an instant, but with each day comes new opportunity. so take heart and Own Your Time!

Key Insights

❖ No matter what your role is in Children's Ministry, you are significant and what you do matters.

❖ Go to staff meetings! If you've ever heard of the saying "out of sight, out of mind," then that's what your Children's Ministry department will become to the senior leadership of your church if you are never a part of staff meetings.

❖ Embrace your failures! They have helped you to become the awesome Kidmin leader you are today. No one is immune to shortcomings and the faster you accept the fact that you're not going to win every time, the quicker you'll position yourself to be a better Children's Minister.

❖ Own your message and be AUTHENTIC! If we want children and their families to truly receive the message we're giving, then we have to be authentic.

❖ Preparing your lesson should not be done the day of. Resist the temptation to cram or procrastinate. Do your homework and get it done!

❖ If you truly want to make an impact in the lives of the next generation, you must be discerning and judicious with the time afforded to you.

❖ Avoid meaningless distractions and set 10 goals a day to help you stay on track.

CHAPTER 5

Understanding The Times

Understanding Challenges to Your Influence

Understanding the challenges to your influence and acting accordingly is vital if you are to be successful in Children's Ministry. Growing up in the church, it used to be that a title or ministry position automatically entitled you to a certain amount of influence and authority. If you wanted to know what 1+1 was, you went to a teacher. Likewise, if you wanted to know how to grow in faith, then you went to a pastor. They were deemed to be the authoritative voices on those matters and if you needed answers, then you needed to go to them. Their titles alone made them the authority. With today's kids, position no longer means much. The truth of the matter is that we're not as in charge as we used to be. Teachers used to be right about everything, but not anymore. The unprecedented access to information brought about by the digital revolution has allowed children to obtain answers by bypassing adults and simply typing their questions into Google.

Beyond this, the age-old "because I said so" response will no longer hold water with today's child who craves, and is easily able to access, credible answers. Kids are not going to stay engaged or value what you say to them just because you're the leader. I will never forget when my daughter stood up in the middle of Children's Church and walked to the back of the room and announced with a loud sigh, "This is boring!" It was horrifying! So after I put on my wig and glasses, I told her, with my fiercest mother laser-eyes, to sit back down and listen to the rest of the lesson. Years ago, my daughter would have been deemed as spoiled, out-of-line, and completely rude. Today, however, pleasing the child has become supremely important, and you may find yourself in the pastor's office if enough children claim that you're dusty and boring. Today, if you want kids to look up to you, you have to give them something to look up to. The age of "I'm a children's pastor so you should listen to me" is over! Title doesn't cut it anymore. It's all about relationships, and if you want to be a true influencer in any space, you better become good at developing them.

The ability to build relationships is vital if you want to have a successful Children's Ministry. Allow me to introduce you to my friend Michael. Michael is a Children's Ministry director who loves kids. He works tirelessly to create a Children's Ministry department that children will love. He has not overcome his natural tendency to be an introvert and regularly avoids talking to people. Therefore, e-mail and occasional in-service advertisements became his primary method of communication to his team and the parents of the church. Michael has struggled for years with having a skeleton crew of volunteers and getting the response he desires from parents. It has left him frustrated time and time again. He is convinced that the main reason people do not help and parents don't respond is due to their lack of spiritual maturity and commitment to the church. So what's Michael's problem? He has leaned too heavily on his title as a director while neglecting the importance of building relationships. Even though he has a heart for children and their families, his lack of attention when it comes to relationship building has cost him greatly. Michael may be a leader on paper, but in the eyes of those around him he has not proven himself to be a leader worthy of following.

In the words of Theodore Roosevelt, "People don't care how much you know until they know how much you care." At the end of the day, showing people that you care grows both your influence and the impact you will make. Title alone does not equal influencer. You have to earn the right to get a call back. You have to earn the right to get parents to do what you ask of them. You have to earn the right to have kids receive you as a valid source. Remember, the more accepted you are by a child, the more open he or she will be to instruction. The same is true for volunteers, parents, and church leadership. Position does give you authority, but it's the lowest level of authority. Influence, however, is of much weightier substance and demands the engagement that we are seeking.

Finding out we had to move to Alabama after a long stint in Chicago was devastating for me. Would I again be forced to church hop until we found a suitable house of worship that would minister to the entire family? After only a few stops we ran into Life Church in Huntsville. I immediately met the Children's Pastor, Kevin Adkins, along with many other staff members. The worship was great, the preaching was dynamic, and the congregation was friendly. All things we had experienced at the other churches we visited. Our children seemed to be happy enough in the Children's Ministry so we decided to momentarily suspend our search. It wasn't until Pastor Kevin invited our family to lunch the following week that something changed. During that lunch I got to hear Kevin and his wife, Tracey, talk about their heart for Children's Ministry. Beyond ministry, we also talked about our lives and the many challenges of raising kids. It was an afternoon filled with fellowship, laughter, and smiles. I walked away so full in body and spirit. That afternoon, Kevin earned my respect and demonstrated to me that he was a leader worth following. Now I know that it is next to impossible to take every family and worker in your ministry out for a meal. However, there are always subtle things you can do to build relationships and show care for those in your ministry. Even the smallest gesture, acknowledgement, or thank you note has the ability to make a huge impact. As Children's Ministry leaders, it is vital that we become better skilled at influencing children, parents, children's ministry workers, and church leadership. Leave the excuses at the door. Be more than a title. Be an influencer.

Understanding Communication Today

In Children's Ministry communication is key. If you want to be a successful Children's Ministry leader, you have to develop the ability to communicate effectively, which includes remaining in step with the evolving methods of communication. In other words, our effectiveness depends upon our ability to keep pace with the ebbs and flows of what's trending when it comes to communication. In view of the diverse communication preferences, it is important that we remain sensitive to the different communication approaches and be strategic in how we reach others. Staying in the know of different communication methods and techniques will not only keep your message relevant but it will make your voice heard.

Having grown up and served in very conservative churches, I am familiar with the traditional methods of communication that churches deploy. In my church, if you wanted people to know something you followed the three main steps:

1. You made a boring plea on Sundays from the pulpit (Hey...I was a kid, you sit and listen to a 5 minute announcement on what the building committee is doing from an old guy named Eddie and see if you don't yawn once or twice);
2. You posted it in the bulletin; and
3. You sent an email.

Follow these three simple steps, and consider your voice heard. Anyone who wanted to target a particular audience might even schedule a meeting at the church, and get this...people actually showed up. The fact of the matter is that times have changed and so has communication. As communication evolves so should our approaches if we hope to stay effective in reaching others.

Allow me to demonstrate the dangers of communication pitfalls through the story of Mary. Mary has just been hired as the Children's Ministry Director at her church. Overjoyed at the opportunity, she is dedicated to growing a healthy Children's Ministry department. Her first order of business is to train her team, so she sets monthly meetings for her volunteers to come together at the church every third Tuesday. She works hard at preparing material for her trainings to ensure that maximum value is added. Unfortunately, despite all of her efforts, She is the only one in attendance. As a result, time is wasted and her materials never see the light of day. She ultimately becomes discouraged and frustrated with her team. She then gives up on all future efforts to train her team and settles for mediocrity. So what was Mary's problem? She was so caught up in her own way of communication that she failed to realize that people are busy! Instead of considering other outlets to reach her team more effectively, Mary pouts, complains, and throws the blame on her volunteers.

Immature leaders exclusively throw the blame on their volunteers instead of assuming some responsibility when matters aren't communicated effectively. However, mature leaders commit themselves to studying communication and learning a variety of avenues in order to maximize their effectiveness. Yes, it's true that back in the day having a standing meeting on the third Tuesday of the month probably worked, and it would have been a fair assessment to question the commitment of those who were not in attendance. But we are living in a day and age where extracurricular activities are at an all-time high, and our children have never been so busy. In addition to the demands of employment, parents find themselves being tossed to and fro by their children's various activities, events, and programming. The reality is that people are busier than ever, and our ministry events may get lost in the shuffle if we aren't carefully communicating them. This rush of activity is no reason to throw in the towel because advancements in technology have also armed us with more tools than ever to effectively reach children, parents, and volunteers.

So what could our friend Mary have done better? She could have given a poll or a survey to gather data on the communication preferences of her volunteers. By inviting her team into the communication process, she would have been able to weed out ineffective methods that consumed so much of her time and effort. Instead of having meetings at the church, she could have hosted monthly conference call training. This would have afforded Mary an opportunity to train while simultaneously offering the flexibility her team so clearly desired. Digital developments like bluetooth, tablets, and social media could have provided convenient access so that her team could listen to the training hands free, from any location, and at the time of their choosing. If the biggest obstacle was the time constraint, she could have created 5 minute training snippets and disseminated them via email, text messaging, or social media. From live web casts to video chatting, the options are endless. When it comes to communicating with others, don't limit yourself to one way. If you find out that one approach isn't working, be creative and switch to another.

More and more churches are using social media as the primary means of communicating with their congregations, teams, and their communities. In fact, it is becoming increasingly rare for a church to not have its own social media page. I have had countless people thank me time and time again for posting videos inviting them to events that they wouldn't have known about otherwise. It could have been easy for me to point out all of the other ways the event was advertised but none of that mattered. The only thing that mattered was that the message was received and they were in attendance. This is why I always recommend that you use multiple approaches when communicating with others. By utilizing different methods of communication, you broaden your reach and boost your effectiveness.

As a voice in Children's Ministry, I have found that one of my most effective communication methods have been through monthly live webinars. As much as I would love to travel the world, having young children and a busy spouse doesn't allow me much room to do so. I also host a Children's Ministry radio show once a month. Through live webinars, and broadcast radio, I have been able to inspire and reach people all over the world in ways I never imagined, and all from the comfort of my own home. With all of the different methods and techniques to reach people, there is still one way that will forever remain timeless and that's face-to-face communication. In person meetings will never lose their value as face-to-face interactions still remain the superior pathway to build relationships, trust, and credibility. I am so passionate about this that I have joined Toastmasters International, an organization dedicated to developing public speaking skills and face-to-face interactions. I have committed myself to constant growth in the area of communication, both digitally and face-to-face, and I encourage you to do the same.

Understanding the New Family Model

This will probably be the shortest section of the book, but don't mistake length as an indicator of importance. I questioned whether to even add this section as it can be a very sensitive topic for some. But regardless of where you stand on certain issues, this topic is one of great significance and, if ignored, could weaken the influence of the church as a whole. If we are to be effective Children's Ministry leaders, then we must be intentional in understanding the new family model that represents the children we minister to week after week.

The truth is that statistically speaking the majority of the kids that fill our Children's Ministries are no longer coming from traditional homes of mom, dad, brother, sister, cat, and dog. Even though there are some, this group is unfortunately growing smaller and smaller as the years progress. In its place, we are seeing more and more children emerge from the following family units:

Single Mom	Single Dad
Dad and Dad	Mom and Mom
Foster Family	Adopted Family
Blended Family	Grandparents

These are the homes our children are growing up in and it is vital that we come up with effective ways to reach them with the hope and transforming power of the gospel.

We were so happy when we moved into our new home in Chicago. The first thing that my husband wanted to do was meet the neighbors. All of our neighbors were absolutely amazing. It wasn't long before we met the neighbors across the street who happened to be a same sex couple. During our time living in Chicago, this couple decided to foster a teenage girl who was abandoned by her grandmother after discovering that she was attracted to girls. My husband and I eventually developed a very strong relationship with her, which resulted in her walking across the street to visit us whenever she pleased. As our relationship flourished, we eventually brought her to church and invited her for a few Bible studies that we hosted at our home. Overtime we shared with her our personal values regarding our faith. Although she eventually moved away from the neighborhood, she continued to consult us for guidance on several issues in her life, including her relationship with God. If we had rejected or otherwise ignored the nontraditional context from which she emerged, our efforts to minister may have been dismissed as insincere or irrelevant.

I am not telling you what to think or what views to uphold. It's up to each church individually to make the decision on where they stand regarding certain issues and how they plan on implementing those values in their ministry settings. However, what I will say is that when it comes to children, I think the words of Christ still ring true, regardless of what families they come from:

> *Jesus said, "Let the little children come to me, and do not hinder them, for the kingdom of heaven belongs to such as these."*

Matthew 19:14 (New International Version)

Understanding the Attack on the Christian Faith

Whether you notice them or not, there are attacks on the Christian Faith with the intentional purpose of undermining the church and its influence. Once upon a time, standing on Christian principles used to be a symbol of pride in the United States. Unfortunately, as time has progressed, the Christian Faith has become a target of discrimination and, for some, persecution. We have witnessed this shift with the removal of prayer from schools.

I will never forget the rash of news stories that emerged after a young boy was dismissed from school after dressing as Jesus for Halloween. The boy was given an ultimatum: either take off the costume or go home, he opted for the latter. It is no secret that school teachers are discouraged from openly discussing their own religious beliefs, which in certain areas can even cost them their jobs. Revealing your Christianity in the public school system is like drawing an *ichthys* in the sand during the Roman Empire under Nero. For those of you unfamiliar with the Greek term, *ichthys*, it is literally translated "fish," and was an acrostic for Jesus Christ, Son of God, and Savior. Early Christians used to identify one another by drawing the symbol of a fish in the sand thereby safely recognizing their shared allegiance to Jesus.

After the publication of my first Christian children's book, Anabel's Light, my daughter Grace asked for permission to take it to school for show and tell. It wasn't until after her teacher read it that she realized that our daughter was from a Christian household. At the school's open house, I saw her teacher's gaze watch for the last parent to leave the room before approaching us. Recognizing we were new to the area, she asked, "Have you all found a church yet?" She then began to make suggestions on potential church homes to consider, including her own. She cautiously confessed her excitement in discovering that Grace was from a strong Christian home, together with her reluctance to mention it as such topics of discussion were frowned upon in the public school. Our conversation came to an abrupt halt as another parent walked into the room.

As a child, my first active encounter with this growing hostility toward the Christian Faith ironically occurred during the holidays. I was so excited to take that picture with Santa Clause. After all these years, I don't even recollect where I was, but I clearly remember my entire class being there. After our polaroids with Santa dried, we were off to the next station to decorate the frames for our pictures. The leader of that station encouraged us to write "Merry X-mas" on our frames so I dutifully followed suit and then commenced bedazzling every crevice of my frame. I was so excited to show my dad when I got home. I'll never forget his response as I sat there glowing with pride waiting to hear how creative I was. As his mouth opened to speak, he immediately said in a loud tone with brows furrowed, "X-mas!" It wasn't until my older sister explained that "X-mas" was essentially taking Christ out of Christmas. Well my second grade mind with the help of my sister interpreted this innocent misstep as a heinous act making me no better than a little red devil with pointy ears and a pitchfork. Nothing like an older sibling to to scar you for life, or at least until you get old enough to not believe everything they say.

My point is that we are at war, and the Christian Faith is under attack in both subtle and not so subtle ways! So if you are a Children's Ministry worker, then part of your responsibility week after week is to equip these little soldiers with messages that encourage them to let their light shine and make disciples. Even so, we cannot underestimate that we are simultaneously dispatching them to environments that frown upon them sharing their faith. In fact doing so could be interpreted as hate speech and land them in detention or worse…suspension. Thank goodness for organizations like Alliance Defending Freedom that fights to preserve the rights and religious freedoms of Christians in a society that seems bent on snuffing faith out. The truth is that there is a very real attack on the Christian Faith and it is vital that we understand that and prepare our children appropriately for battle!

Key Insights

❖ Choose to be an influencer and a leader worthy of following.

❖ Find creative ways to build relationships with your team.

❖ Consider multiple ways to communicate effectively with your children's parents and volunteers.

❖ Don't play the blame game when it comes to your team. Just choose to be a better leader.

❖ If we are to be effective Children's Ministry leaders, then we must be intentional in understanding the new family model that represents the children we minister to week after week.

❖ Talk to your senior leadership and create a plan to effectively reach children coming from non-traditional family models in your ministry.

❖ Know that the Christian Faith is under attack. Prepare your kids for battle.

CHAPTER 6

Engaging Technology

Do you remember when people used to answer a ringing phone with no clue of the caller's identity? Do you recall the time when driving to any new destination without a map was unthinkable? Or can you imagine an era where family members did not have to compete with television, tablets, or telephones to communicate with one another? Well…those days are gone; and if we want to remain relevant in Children's Ministry, then we need to put on our wetsuits and ride this digital wave. It's unavoidable. The digital age is here and it's not going anywhere! Technological advancements are ever-growing and transforming the way we do everything from reading our bibles to learning in schools. The bottom line is that our children are growing up in a world dominated by technology, and if we want to stay connected with them then we better plug in

Start With an Open Mind

So what is your mindset towards the digital age? As far as we've come, I believe that there are still too many churches that have yet to fully embrace digital technology. When it comes to the digital age, we should maintain a willingness to leverage it to achieve our ultimate goal of reaching boys and girls with the hope of Jesus Christ. So what stops us from connecting with these digital natives? Since the beginning of time, there have been tensions between one generation and the next concerning various topics, technological developments are no exception.

We've all heard that age old saying from Uncle Jim, "In my day and age we didn't need to (fill-in-blank)." This typically followed a speech about how right their generation was, and how wrong, corrupt, or lazy the subsequent generation has turned out to be. And then that fateful day comes when we wake up, look in the mirror, and realize we've become Uncle Jim! Now don't get me wrong, Uncle Jim is great. He's definitely the life of the party every year around the holidays, but Uncle Jim got one thing wrong. Uncle Jim was closeminded and tried to fit a newer generation in the box of an older one. Jesus himself warns us of the folly of approaching a new age with an antiquated mindset:

> *"No one sews a patch of unshrunk cloth on an old garment, for the patch will pull away from the garment, making the tear worse. Neither do people pour new wine into old wineskins. If they do, the skins will burst; the wine will run out and the wineskins will be ruined. No, they pour new wine into new wineskins, and both are preserved."*

Matthew 9:16-17 (New International Version).

If we close our minds to the impact the Digital Age is having on our kids, then we may find that our old school methods have the unintended consequence of repelling them away from us, our churches, and our message. We waste so much time arguing over which methods are "appropriate" that we often miss the mark entirely. By way of example, if one person chooses to wash the dishes by hand while another washes the dishes in the dishwasher, don't both sets of dishes end up clean? A decision to completely discard all digital technology in our Children's Ministry departments may cause the next generation to dismiss the church as old, stodgy, and boring. It is vital that we are open minded and intentional in leveraging digital technology for the glory of God so that our message is amplified and our relevance maintained.

The Best Digital Trainers

Admittedly, it seems as if technological advancements are happening at the speed of light, but the same technologies have also afforded us such access to information that we don't have to be fearful or intimidated by them. Rest assured there are plenty of resources to help you navigate these torrential digital waters. Like anything, if you're willing to invest sufficient energy, money, and time, you too can master this digital age. But with the plethora of websites, tutorials, and resources available, it is easy to overlook the greatest little trainers that are right under our very noses...our kids!

For example, when I started my own social media platform I was determined to do videos to really make myself stand out, but I just wasn't happy with the finished product. The videos conveyed the message well enough, but they simply lacked the kick of personality that I envisioned for my platform. I knew exactly what I wanted but did not possess the skillset to achieve the vision. Guess who did? My 12 year old goddaughter Tatiana was a wiz at creating videos in minutes that were fully equipped with all the quirky sounds and side effects a girl could want. Tatiana and I had a great time creating fun videos together that entire summer, which was particularly special because it was our last season together before relocating to Alabama. I learned so much from her. I will never forget how she surprised us with one last video that she secretly created to say goodbye. I don't think there was a dry eye in the room.

It turns out that my summer tutorial in video editing was also an amazing time of bonding between me and my goddaughter. The point is that children are some of the best teachers when it comes to technology. They are early adopters and experienced users of the video games, apps, and social media platforms that are currently trending. If you want to know the hottest apps, devices, and websites that are of most interest to the next generation, then why not ask them? In fact, I have found that asking kids about their digital devices and games is one of the best ways to reach and connect with them. There's nothing kids love more than grown-ups asking them for their advice. It's an incredible experience for them and it builds their self-esteem significantly. On Sunday mornings we regularly remind our kids to not "*let anyone look down on you because you are young*" (1 Timothy 4:12), but rarely give them an opportunity to serve as examples for us or our ministries. Why not? The truth is that our children do have a lot to offer, particularly in the realm of digital technology. Don't make the mistake of underestimating these bite-sized digital trainers and all they have to offer those who seek to better understand this digital age.

Sacrifice is the Name of the Game

This is a tough one guys but sacrifice is the name of the game if we truly want to become skilled at all things technology, or at least some form of tech. Our first step in integrating digital technology into our Children's Ministries is learning about digital technology! It's just as simple as that. At the end of the day, there's no such thing as faking it until you make it. You can try, but your cover will inevitably be blown if you have not put in the necessary work to gain a basic understanding of what technologies are appropriate for your ministry. No matter what area you want to excel in, some form of sacrifice needs to be made to acquire a skill. So if you want to up your skills in technology, then get ready to put your work boots on. Everyone has to put in some form of work to become better at anything, and the more work you put in the better you will become.

YouTube

There are a variety of books out there to choose from that can help you on your journey to becoming more tech savvy. From audio options to video recordings, the possibilities are endless. But one of my favorite sources of digital training is YouTube. I love searching topics and devouring all the How-to videos that pop up after each inquiry. Need help on how to use snapchat, play Fortnite, or what is Fortnite?! Then YouTube will be your friend. I cannot tell you how many tips I gained on how to use certain apps and other forms of software.

Being a Proactive Learner

Of course, as I discussed previously, utilize the young digital natives that are around you. They will be happy to help. However, I caution you to not completely forego actual learning yourself. I can't tell you how many Children's Ministry leaders I know who have done this. Instead of learning the skills they need, they simply assign technical tasks to those who are more knowledgeable in a certain area to hold down the fort. Don't get me wrong. This is not a bad thing. I always encourage leaders to delegate roles. I believe a healthy Children's Ministry department reflects a diverse group of people who all use their different gifts and talents to make the department better. However, this can be a little more complicated when it comes to digital technology. For instance, if we have dedicated ourselves to having a tech-infused Children's Ministry, then we would be well served to avoid relying entirely on the one high school student that may or may not be there on Sunday. I have seen this happen, and it is not pretty. Let me tell you, there is no amount of stalling that can avoid the chaos that ensues when a media-led children's church has no one to direct the media.

Stick With It

As I mentioned earlier, sacrifice is the name of the game. A significant investment of time will be required in order to become tech savvy. One time it took me 3 hours just to navigate through a popular app called musically; and let me tell you, the product I came up with was mediocre at best. But today I am so much better because practice makes perfect. I know what you're thinking, as if our lives aren't busy enough, now you're asking me to sacrifice the time I don't have to learn how to do something I have no clue on how to do. And my answer is a resounding yes! At the end of the day, we all make time for what's important to us and if connecting with the next generation is important to you, then this sacrifice will be well worth it.

Now I'm not asking you to quit your job to stay home and play Fortnite all day, but what I am asking you to do is to be willing to give up some activities for the purposes of enhancing your skills in digital media. And stick with it. It can be a slow grueling process to learn how to do anything that doesn't come naturally, but don't give up. You got this! Stay focused on the ultimate goal, which is to reach children more effectively with the gospel message of Christ. Refuse to quit, even when it gets hard. Thinking back to my college days, I will never forget the statistics class I took one summer. As soon as the teacher opened his mouth and began to point to the board, everything started to get fuzzy. I can remember looking at all the numbers and charts wondering how in the world I was going to pass that class. It all felt so foreign to me. It seemed like every new formula and graph went over my head. If I wasn't sure whether I was comprehending the material, the failing grade on my first quiz was proof positive that I was not.

My confusion led to frustration and I began to hate the class because of it. It wasn't until I stopped and re-evaluated the greater purpose behind why I needed to take the class that my performance recovered. I realized that I needed to pass that class if I was going to be able to graduate from the university. It was at that moment that I decided to hunker down and do the best that I could to learn the material. I asked some of my classmates for help. Their assistance and accountability became invaluable to me. With only one quarter remaining until graduation, I was determined to master statistics. I stayed up late, got up early, and spent time at the local coffee shops while my friends hung out. I'll never forget when a friend who was in the class texted me to tell me their grade and to see what I got. I sheepishly went to the campus website, scrolled down to the Esther Moreno Grades Section, and squinted my eyes. When I opened them wide enough to see anything, I took a deep breathe, and low and behold there was my B+ shining like a diamond ring in the sun. I had done it! And so can you!

It doesn't matter where you are in your understanding of this digital age. Through hard work, focus, and dedication, you too can develop the necessary skills to talk all things digital with the best of them. Remember practice makes perfect! The more you practice, the better you will become. Think of practice like exercise. The more you exercise, the stronger your muscles will become, and before you know it, what used to take your breath away, doesn't even touch the surface of what you can accomplish now. When it comes to digital technology, Tech Researcher, Toyoji Matsumoto, said, "Do it 1,000 times 'til it becomes natural — then do it another 1,000 times!" The best way to learn a language is to immerse yourself into the culture. The same is true for digital media. Make it a point not to beat yourself up if you get some things wrong along the way. It takes time for certain skills to become second nature so show yourself some grace. I will never forget when my husband went to Mexico on a missions' trip and made the rookie mistake of confusing the phrase *"tengo calor"* ("It is hot" from a temperature perspective) with *"estoy caliente"* ("I am hot" from a sexual perspective). He hadn't realized his error until someone kindly took him to the side and explained to him the difference. He was horrified. Today, my husband is fluent in Spanish and has very few problems keeping pace with native speakers. So whatever you do, stick with it, show yourself some grace, celebrate every win no matter how small, and please, please, please DON'T QUIT!

Engaging Tech to Connect

To the Jews I became like a Jew, to win the Jews. To those under the law I became like one under the law (though I myself am not under the law), so as to win those under the law. To those not having the law I became like one not having the law (though I am not free from God's law but am under Christ's law), so as to win those not having the law. To the weak I became weak, to win the weak. I have become all things to all people so that by all possible means I might save some.

1 Corinthians 9:20-22 (New International Version)

The Apostle Paul was someone who knew the times. He used current events to connect with people for the purposes of leading them to Christ. His ability to immerse himself into the culture of the day allowed him to more effectively connect with his audience. Similarly, if we want to connect with children, it is of vital importance that we do the same. We must not lose sight that digital media presents an amazing avenue to connect with the hearts and minds of our children. Parents and Children's Ministry leaders often know that there is a very real chasm between our world and the world of a child. We must not allow the enemy to widen this gap by robbing us of the opportunity to connect with our kids through the avenue of digital media. It is vital that we stay connected with what's current if we want our message to remain relevant in the hearts and minds of our children. When we infuse things like apps, video games, and social media into our Children's Ministries, it expands our reach and impact among the digital natives that populate our Children's Ministries.

I was so impressed when I dropped my daughter off in the kid's area at one of the local churches we were visiting after our relocation to Alabama. The first thing I noticed when walking in the Kidmin waiting room was that the walls were dotted with little screens each equipped with its own gaming system. Beyond the traditional Kidmin icebreakers, there were children playing video games on each one of the gaming systems. I also noticed some of the older children spread out on beanbag chairs playing on their phones. After about 10-15 minutes, the kids were asked to clean up and gather for the main children's church service. I can remember thinking to myself, wow, video games at church! Do you know how many people would go into cardiac arrest at the mere thought of video games in church! I had to discover what inspired the room layout and vision for the space. After sitting down with the children's pastor, I was not surprised to hear his answer: To Connect. His answer was brilliant in its simplicity! He continued, "I don't know all there is to know about digital technology. In fact, I'm still learning. But I do know that when the kids walk in on Sunday and see those video games it speaks a message to them that simple words can't.

It tells them that we see them, we care about the things that matter to them, and that makes all the difference."

Like Paul was called to the Gentiles, we have been called to Children's Ministry. Paul knew very well the challenges confronting that generation. He was keenly aware of the different idols, wolves in sheep's clothing, and other threats that were pervasive among the regions. Undoubtedly, all of this information was of great benefit to his ministry. But it was likely his willingness to "become all things to all men" (I Corinthians 19:22), was his greatest advantage in demonstrating his care for people. Kids, too, must know that you authentically care about them before they will hear what you have to say. And if kids, as digital natives, care about the digital age, then so should you.

Digitally Enhanced Children's Ministries

Digital Media provides an opportunity to present your message in fun and engaging ways. Please don't sleep on this. Choose to bring your message to life. Time and time again, I have personally observed a sense of excitement around the use of digital media in our Sunday school lessons. Even if limited to an opening video clip, this excitement tends to last throughout the entire lesson. You can keep the momentum going by including references to new movies or video games that the kids love. Drop in some of the latest dance trends while you're worshipping. I cannot tell you the authority and respect one is given after doing a dance move that is popular with the kids. When the kids found out I could floss after a Fortnite dance battle, I could have told them Jesus commanded them to eat 10 banana peppers a day and they would have believed me! So leverage the latest trends to make your message come alive. Bottom line, make it your business to know what the kids care about.

Utilize videos, apps, and games in your curriculum. There are some great bible apps out there created for children. So use them, and let the kids use them. Use clips and videos to illustrate your bible message. A variety of curriculums on the market have already recognized the powerful impact of presenting messages using technology and come pre-packaged with a variety of applicable digital presentations. Choose to personalize your message by creating your own video. They say a picture is worth a thousand words, so a video must be worth a million. There are so many Children's Ministry departments who sponsor children from all over the world. How revolutionary would it be to actually FaceTime or show video footage of the child your ministry was sponsoring? This is just one example, but my point is BE CREATIVE in your approach when it comes to engaging digital technology into your Children's Ministry.

Utilizing digital technology in our Children's Ministries is not limited to our Sunday lessons. Social media has made it possible for many Children's Ministries to witness, create virtual communities, and expand our communication channels with parents and volunteers. Tools like Google Doc enable church leaders to more efficiently recruit and schedule the volunteer assistance they need. Digital check-in/registration systems bring our ministries into the 21st Century so that we can leverage the data to do things like immediately identify and address any lags in attendance. In addition to all of this, training has never been easier. With the click of a button, you can gain access to some of the greatest minds Children's Ministry has to offer through virtual trainings and webcasts. The options are endless and the opportunities are massive so happy reaching!

Key Insights

❖ Be open-minded when it comes to digital technology. If we close our minds to the impact the Digital Age is having on our kids, then we may find that our old school methods have the unintended consequence of repelling them away from us, our churches, and our message.

❖ Don't underestimate the children around you, these digital trainers have a lot to teach us about digital technology, so ask them!

❖ To enhance your digital literacy, consider resources like books, audio options, and self-help videos found on various media platforms such as YouTube.

❖ Be intentional about learning the basic skills of digital media around you. This can be a daunting task but no matter what, DON'T QUIT!

❖ When we infuse things like popular apps, video games, and social media into our Children's Ministries, it expands our reach and impact among the digital natives that populate our churches.

❖ Consider using digital technology as an organizational tool to more effectively communicate, coordinate, and identify trends within your Children's Ministry.

CHAPTER 7

Breaking the Mold

One of the greatest things about Children's Ministry is that you can break the mold without breaking the rules. What I mean by this is that you can be a dynamic trend setter that stands out and creates massive impact without being known as the "rule breaker." Following the rules is important; and like we teach our kids, the rules help to keep us safe. So what are rules? Rules are the principles that guide the decisions we make. Principles are non-negotiable. These fundamental truths serve as the foundation for why we do what we do. In our case, that truth would be our doctrinal beliefs in Christ that guide everything we do in our Children's Ministries. While these doctrinal beliefs are immutable, the methods we choose to communicate them may vary.

Stated differently, principles remain constant, but methods can be tweaked. For instance, a principle might be prayer. As Christians, prayer is the way we communicate with God. It's also a way we develop a deeper relationship with Him. It is vital that we teach our kids how to commune with the Father through prayer. However, the methods we use to teach our children how to pray can vary from one generation to the next. Like prayer, preaching the Word of God to children is a non-negotiable principle. But the methods, means and ways to do so are potentially limitless. One leader may use an illustrative model while another may choose digital methods or other formats to get the same message across.

One of Children's Ministries greatest challenges is the temptation to convert methods into rules. Unfortunately, some people are so stuck in their own way of doing things that they completely reject the possibility that it can be done in another, and potentially better, way. These people are small thinkers, and are often intimidated or fearful of the ideas of newer leaders. Rather than evaluating each method, idea, or approach on its own merits, they force, cajole, or manipulate others to stick to the status quo at all costs. This limited worldview is not new to our day, but is the very same Pharisaical attitude that sought to crucify Christ. If our Lord and Savior combatted small mindedness to achieve the call of God, so can we. Fear not because great Kidmin leaders can creatively break the mold without compromising core principles. They are driven by passion and vision rather than the opinions of others.

Uncommon Children's Ministry Leader

Hear me when I say this. You can't be common in Children's Ministry! People who refuse to rock the boat are common. They are your typical, familiar, ordinary leaders. You don't really expect anything big out of them because they are your standard leader who usually focuses more on maintaining a Children's Ministry space rather than refining it. The common Children's Ministry leader goes nowhere. So choose to be uncommon. At the end of the day, great success is uncommon, and, therefore, rarely tasted by common Children's Ministry leaders.

The uncommon Children's Ministry leader cannot be a one-man show. Yet so many Children's Ministry leaders fall into this category. When I was first hired for a position in Children's Ministry, I was determined to prove that I had what it took to take the ministry to the next level, or at least prevent it from sinking to the ground. I had no clue what I was doing! I rubbed shoulders with the most difficult people and tried to please them by producing every request asked of me. I stayed up late and woke up early setting up and tearing down. I personally made

myself responsible for all things children's ministry at our church. And
with this distorted view of excellence, I ran myself into the ground! Do
you see the same key word here... It's "I." In case you haven't heard this
enough, there's no "I" in team. Uncommon leaders recognize this. Yes,
God has called each and every one of us, but he never called for us to
do it alone! If this has ever been you, don't beat yourself up about! It
happens to the best of us. It's never too late to become the uncommon
leader you were created to be!

Even Moses struggled with the "one man show" syndrome. In
Exodus 18, when Moses' father-in-law paid him a visit, he offered Moses
some much needed advice after observing the crushing workload upon
his son-in-law's shoulders:

> Moses' father-in-law replied, "What you are doing is not
> good. You and these people who come to you will only wear
> yourselves out. The work is too heavy for you; you cannot
> handle it alone...
>
> But select capable men from all the people—men who
> fear God, trustworthy men who hate dishonest gain—and
> appoint them as officials over thousands, hundreds, fifties
> and tens...That will make your load lighter, because they
> will share it with you.

Exodus 18: 17-18a; 21 (New International Version)

YOU CAN'T DO IT ALONE! Nor should you feel like you have
to. There are people around you that God has called to help you. It's
your job to weed out the good from the not so good and ASK, ASK,
ASK!!!! Don't know people? GET TO KNOW THEM! You can't build
strong volunteer teams hiding in a corner! Trust me, I know! So get
off of the sideline and into the game! Get out there and be relational.
And never say "no" on behalf of someone else! Stop making excuses in
your head on why you can't ask someone who you think would be an
awesome Kidmin ministry partner to join your team. Attitudes like that

self-sabotage your efforts before you even get started. Stop and think about all the areas where you could use a little help. The help you need isn't always in the classroom. For example, someone who may not be willing to lead in a classroom may jump at the chance to help set up and tear down one before and after service. No job is too small and every job is just as significant as the next! So be bold, be courageous, be uncommon, and go get those God has already assigned to help you!

Continual Growth

The uncommon Children's Ministry leader understands the importance of continual learning and development. In the midst of the hustle and bustle of our Kidmin responsibilities, it can be easy to brush this concept of continual growth off until a more opportune time. Unfortunately that time never comes for most leaving many feeling like the proverbial hamster on the wheel. Uncommon leaders are always committed to growth and a lifetime of learning, not just in the area of children's ministry but in every area of their lives. I love visiting other Children's Ministries and seeing all of the wonderful things they are doing to reach the next generation for Christ. I also make it a habit to read 3 books a month. One of those books is dedicated to how I can be an awesome Kidmin leader. The other books are generally dedicated to another area of my life where I wish to grow in like prayer or marriage. The key here isn't just to fill your head with knowledge, but to be more intentional in the application of that newly-acquired knowledge. If you've learned a fun tip on how to bring your leaders together, then try it! Every ministry is unique, and what works for one may not work for another, but you never know what tip may transform your ministry.

Make Your Voice Heard

The uncommon leader sees beyond the urgent. They are willing to make the necessary investments to inspire parents. The uncommon leader isn't afraid to address senior leadership. Dealing with parents and senior leadership can be a challenging endeavor. Sometimes it can get downright uncomfortable. In order to be an uncommon leader, you have to get comfortable with being uncomfortable. You have to be willing to be a rebel when the time calls for it, and, if necessary, to flip over a few tables. Now don't get me wrong, I am a firm believer that we should always strive to keep peace with the senior leadership in our churches. But it is also important for uncommon leaders to be bold and willing to speak truth to the senior leadership when they are misunderstood.

One of the greatest complaints I hear from Children's Ministry leaders is the lack of understanding among senior leadership concerning the weekly operations of the Children's Ministry department. Uncommon leaders don't wallow in misunderstood self-pity. They understand that it is their job to sell what needs to happen in the Children's Ministry to their senior leadership. It is natural to not completely understand the inner workings of other ministry areas beyond your own. As passionate and hardworking as we are, we will never truly understand the great weight and responsibility of the Senior Pastor. Why? Because we're not Senior Pastors! The only way we can begin to understand is through our relationship with a Senior Pastor. An uncommon leader does not expect for their ministry colleagues to be mind-readers, but instead is gracious and willing to help people understand.

The uncommon leader realizes and embraces the fact that they are an ambassador of the Children's Ministry department. They understand that you catch more flies with honey than vinegar, and approach situations with a keen sense of diplomacy. Uncommon leaders don't come into staff meetings like wrecking balls. They know that to be invited back to the table requires a level of wise pragmatism. As a Children's Ministry leader, part of your job is to convince the leadership in your church of the significance of Children's Ministry. Don't waste it. If you are given a seat at the table, make sure that you don't make the leaders regret having invited you in the first place. This reminds me of a colleague of mine who really optimized her seat at the table. Because she had the ear of the leadership, she was able to bring many of her visions to fruition, which included children's ministry gardens, art camps, and more. Part of her effectiveness was that she attended every staff meeting prepared to discuss the needs of the Children's Ministry while genuinely supporting the needs of others.

Celebrating the Skills of Others

Uncommon leaders are not threatened by quality people and are comfortable working with highly skilled individuals. There is nothing worse than an insecure leader. In my own experience, I have suffered the sting of working with someone who was intimidated by my energy alone and the attention it often got me. As the insecurity grew, so did their lack of support in everything I did. I was extremely limited in what I could do there as a result. To this day, I believe God graciously pulled me out of that situation because he knew he had built me for more. Unfortunately, many of my gifts could not be seen through the cloud of one person's insecurity. However, I was so grateful for each and every individual who recognized some of my talents during that season, and pulled me out of the shadows so that I could let my light shine. It saddened me at the time to think of the amazing duo we could have been and the massive impact we could have made on the Children's Ministry in the absence of those insecurities. As uncommon leaders, we must be more concerned with the health of our Children's Ministry departments than our own popularity. It's only when we become confident in our own abilities and what they bring to the table that we can truly appreciate and celebrate the skills and talents of others.

Protecting Leaders from Burnout

Uncommon leaders know how to schedule workers and recognize the need to give people breaks to prevent burnout. Your volunteers are one of your most valuable resources. They should be nurtured. Some volunteers legitimately feel bad and won't tell you when they need a break. There are a variety of churches that build breaks into their programs by limiting the weeks one is allowed to serve per month. At one of my churches, we had a practice of bringing in an entirely new team of leaders for the summer every year so that the leaders that served during the school year could enjoy a break. Even with breaks, circumstances can occur that will knock the wind out of some of your people. An uncommon leader stays connected with what's going on with their leaders, and learns to identify and address signs of burnout. Uncommon leaders are not afraid to stop what not's working. They evaluate, assess, and make the necessary decisions that need to be made. In addition to this, uncommon leaders aren't afraid to demote those who need to be demoted and promote those who deserve to be promoted.

Protecting Your Spiritual Health

The most important attribute that an uncommon leader possesses is a healthy spiritual life. So many Children's Ministry leaders struggle with anxiety and burnout. Why? Because God is our center! When we replace our center with anything else, even ministry, it causes everything in our life to be off kilter. Uncommon leaders know that their spiritual health is of vital importance if they are going to successfully lead or serve in a Children's Ministry department. They know that they can't afford to put their relationship with God on the back burner. The uncommon leader spends regular time meditating on God's word in order to stay grounded in His truth. They submit to it and strive to walk in accordance with His will. They pour out their heart before God in prayer, regularly seeking Him for their strength, peace, and joy. Uncommon leaders are not cynical because they trust God in all circumstances. They don't sweat the small stuff. They are determined to spread love wherever they go because they know the supreme importance of being a visible reflection of Christ. We are constantly bombarded with to-dos, responsibilities, and ever increasing expectations that have a tendency to crowd out our personal relationships with God. Be a leader who breaks the mold and guard your spiritual health. The health of your Children's Ministry department depends on it.

Key Insights

- ❖ Avoid converting methods into rules.
- ❖ Don't take on more than you were called to bear. Delegate, Delegate, Delegate!
- ❖ Commit yourself to a lifetime of learning not only in Children's Ministry but in every area of your life.
- ❖ Gracefully make your voice heard to the senior leadership of your church.
- ❖ Go to staff meetings prepared to discuss the needs of your Children's Ministry while genuinely supporting the needs of others.
- ❖ Learn to recognize when your leaders need a break and give them one.
- ❖ Celebrate the gifts and talents of others.
- ❖ Don't put your spiritual health on the backburner. Be intentional in investing in your relationship with God.

CONCLUSION

I hope that this book has blessed you as much as it has blessed me writing it. Remember, your success hinges on knowing yourself, knowing your audience, being prepared, owing your message, understanding the times, engaging technology, and choosing to be a leader who breaks the mold. If you have discovered any principles in this book that have served to enhance your Children's Ministry department, I would love to hear about it. Drop me a message at childsheart83@gmail.com.

The truth is that the concept of Children's Ministry is changing. The methods we use to reach children and young people has to be evaluated from multiple angles. Examining our programs and strategies for reaching kids is going to be the difference maker if we are to be successful in reaching the next generation for Christ. In this book, I have provided you with key principles that, if carefully considered and applied will help you win in your efforts to reach young people. Remember, information received and not applied is useless. Children can be reached. You have been appointed for such a time as this to reach them effectively.

Embrace the opportunity that has been given to you. Decide now to excel in all that you do. Celebrate every triumph. Have grace for yourself if you fail as we all do. No matter what, choose to enjoy the journey on the way to where you're going. Believe in yourself and know you were made for this! Press on Kidmin Extraordinaire…press on!

Brothers and sisters, I do not consider myself yet to have taken hold of it. But one thing I do: Forgetting what is behind and straining toward what is ahead, I press on toward the goal to win the prize for which God has called me heavenward in Christ Jesus.

Philippians 3:13-14 (New International Version)

HEAR WHAT PEOPLE ARE SAYING ABOUT ESTHER MORENO…

Esther Moreno is being used by God in our generation to bring new insights and leadership to Children's Ministry. Discover the powerful secrets of how to move your ministry forward and make a lasting impact on future generations. Esther's passion for Children's Ministry is contagious and as real as it gets. You will not be disappointed.

Kevin Adkins
Children's Pastor
Life Church Huntsville
Huntsville, Alabama

If you are interested in remaining a participant in stale, stagnant, "same as your mama's" Children's Ministry, don't read this book. But if you are eager to break the chains that are holding your Children's Ministry captive, you hold in your hands the keys to unlocking the future of Kidmin. In "Children's Ministry Moving Forward," Esther Moreno will challenge you to courageously step outside the box of traditional practices, aiming your influence right at the heart of kids as you carry out her universal principles in easy to replicate, practical ways.

John Allen
Senior Pastor
St. Stephens United Methodist Church
Yazoo City, Mississippi

The ministry to children has seen tremendous growth and expansion, but there is still much left to do. As we look toward greater advancement in reaching children for Jesus Christ, Esther Moreno's book, "Children's Ministry Moving Forward," gives tremendous insight on how we get there. Understanding the opportunities we have to disciple the next church is vital in Kingdom legacy. Preparation and positioning ourselves as we build stronger cores in Children's Ministry will allow us greater access to reach children. Recognizing the environment and times in which children live will serve as a catalyst to connect to a sometimes seemingly unconnected generation. Being courageous to break religious molds will allow us to engage in what the Holy Spirit speaks and act on it. These are all brilliant strategies, but knowing what to do and how to do it is not so easy. I am thankful for Esther's book, because it offers practical, yet cutting-edge solutions and concepts to help us achieve this kind of effectiveness in the ministry to children.

Rosemary Winbush
Pastor of Oasis Children and Preteen Ministry
The Bethel Church
Jacksonville, Florida

Esther has dedicated her life to helping children discover who they are in Christ. If you are looking to raise your leadership lid in Children's Ministry, this is the book for you. "Children's Ministry Moving Forward: A Healthy Kidmin Perspective" will help you become more than a volunteer or chief ministry planner. By raising your leadership lid, you will be able to empower others to be disciple-makers.

Bo Harrington
Southeast Kids Equipping Pastor
Southeast Christian Church
Louisville, Kentucky

Esther Moreno's life sings with a passion and love for Jesus Christ and the children he created and died to save. Following the example of Jesus, Esther has dedicated her life to sacrificially serving the youngest members of the body of Christ. In reading these pages, you will not only benefit from her experience and expertise, you will also find yourself caught up in her passion for all things Kidmin!

Chadwick Kellenbarger
Executive Pastor
Journey Christian Church
Greeley, Colorado

Esther Moreno is one of the most effective Kidmin leaders I have worked with in congregations both large and small, rural and urban in the course of over three decades. Her wisdom, experience and love for God's people come pouring off the pages of this must-read narrative of what it takes to embrace dynamic and successful leadership in Children's Ministry. Esther's insight into Kidmin will encourage your own ministry and strengthen your faith in what God will do through you.

Rev. Clinton G. Roberts
Senior Pastor
Knox Presbyterian Church
Chicago, Illinois

CPSIA information can be obtained
at www.ICGtesting.com
Printed in the USA
FFHW022112141218
49891629-54488FF

9 781984 571601